THE NATION'S FIRST FAMILY

RETROSPECT 1965

ACE BOOKS, INC.
1120 Avenue of the Americas
New York, New York 10036

Printed in the U.S.A.

CONTENTS

SUMMARY-JANUARY 1964

NATIONAL

The Republican Senator from Arizona, Barry Morris Goldwater, formally announced (Jan. 3) that he would seek his party's nomination for the Presidency of the United States. He declared himself a candidate in the presidential primaries in New Hampshire, Illinois, Oregon and California . . . Senator Goldwater's first pronouncement of policy as a candidate for the Presidency was that if elected he would threaten to break relations with the Soviet Union unless the Soviets yielded to justified U.S. demands . . . **Margaret Chase Smith**, Republican Senator from Maine, later in the month (Jan. 27), became the first woman candidate for the Republican presidential nomination by announcing that she would enter the New Hampshire primary.

A meeting with the Pope was suggested by President Lyndon Baines Johnson (Jan. 5) sometime in the future at a place to be specified.

The 88th Congress reconvened (Jan. 7) and the next day heard President Johnson ask for a budget of $97.9 billion, a cut of $500 million from the '63 budget . . . War on poverty was the high point of the President's budget which pointed out that 30 million Americans belonged to families with incomes of less than $2,000 a year and that three million single people received incomes of less than $1,500 a year.

The Rules Committee of the House of Representatives under Chairman Howard Smith yielded to pressure and began hearings on the most comprehensive civil rights bill ever proposed to Congress.

The danger to health in the smoking of cigarettes was officially confirmed by the Surgeon General of the U.S. Public Health Service in a 150,000 word report. Heavy cigarette smokers, the report stated, have a mortality rate from lung cancer 1,000 per cent greater than non-smokers.

The first national labor contract was negotiated (Jan. 15) by James Hoffa's International Brotherhood of Teamsters. Some 16,000 truckers agreed to pay 400,000 teamsters increases in wages amounting to more than $400 million over a period of 35 months . . . **The 1963 rise in prices** of 1.7 per cent was the largest since 1958 . . . Average factory wages rose to a record $2.50 an hour with the average weekly wage rising to a record $105 per week.

Theodore C. Sorensen, closest to the late President John F. Kennedy of the White House staff, became the first holdover from the Kennedy administration to tender his resignation (Jan. 15) to President Johnson. Mr. Sorensen resigned to write a book about his former chief . . . **Arthur M. Schlesinger Jr.**, most controversial member of the late president's staff, handed in his resignation a few days later announcing that he also intended to write a book . . . **Ed Murrow** resigned as chief of the United States Information Agency (Jan. 21) for reasons of health and was succeeded by **Carl T. Rowan**, Negro diplomat and newspaperman . . . **Lt. Col. John H. Glenn**, first American to orbit the earth in space, resigned as an astronaut to seek the Democratic senatorial nomination in Ohio.

A space craft with the heaviest payload in history was launched by the U.S. (Jan. 29). The Saturn missile, 16 stories high, carried a 20,000 pound payload, far exceeding the heaviest payload of 14,292 pounds ever rocketed into space by the Soviet Union . . . **A Ranger space craft**, designed to crash land on the moon and televise pictures back to earth, was launched by the U.S. one day later.

The investigation of the business activities of **Robert G. Baker** as Secretary to the Democratic Senate Majority by the Senate Rules Committee produced testimony about a gift made by a friend of Baker's to the then Senate Majority leader, Lyndon B. Johnson.

The 24th Amendment to the Constitution, banning state poll taxes, was ratified (Jan. 23) when South Dakota became the 38th state to approve it . . . **The U.S. Supreme Count** ruled that conscientious objectors to military service did not need to prove their belief in a Supreme Being . . . A New York State Supreme Court justice ruled that the state must supply auto license plates without the advertisement for the New York World's Fair of '64 and '65 to any motorist who objected to the ad.

Plans for the world's tallest buildings, twin towers 1350 feet high, were announced (Jan. 18) for a new trade center in downtown New York. The towers, standing on a five acre plot, will soar eight stories and 100 feet higher than the Empire State Building. Construction will begin in 1965 and be completed in 1970.

Byron De La Beckwith went on trial (Jan. 31) for the murder of Medgar Evers, Negro executive of the National Association for the Advancement of Colored People, in Jackson, Mississippi . . . **Igor Cassini**, former syndicated society columnist and public relations man, was given a six-month suspended sentence and fined $10,000 for failing to register as an agent for the Dominican government of dictator Trujillo.

INTERNATIONAL

Pope Paul VI broke several precedents and long established traditions on a three day visit to the Holy Land (Jan. 4-6). He became the first pope to travel by plane, the first pope to meet with a Patriarch of the Eastern Orthodox Church (Benedictos of Jerusalem) in five centuries, first pope to leave Italy since Pius VII in 1809, first pope to be received by an Arab king in an Arab country (Jordan), the first pope to visit Israel, the first to follow in the footsteps of Christ from condemnation to Calvary. The journey, during which the Pope met with Ecumenical Patriarch Athenagoras of Constantinople (Istanbul), head of the Eastern Orthodox Church, was made to advance the cause of Christian unity.

The Berlin Wall, which the East Germans had opened for the Christmas season to some 1,250,000 West German visitors was closed again January 5.

The Central Intelligence Agency reported (Jan. 7) that Russia's economic growth had faltered to 2.5 per cent per year for 1962 and 1963, well below the growth rate of the U.S.

In South Viet Nam, a triumvirate of generals headed by Major General Ton That Dinh took over (Jan. 7) the government of the country . . . The triumvirate fell before the end of the month (Jan. 29) when military dissidents led by Major General Nguyen Khanh seized power.

Venezuela formally accused Cuba (Jan. 2) before the Organization of American States (OAS) of carrying on subversive activities in her territory . . . **Bloody rioting flared in Panama** (Jan. 9) when high school students in U.S. Zone raised a U.S. flag without an accompanying Panamanian flag in violation of an agreement between the two countries. Seven were killed and 75 injured. President Roberto F. Chiari suspended relations with the U.S. pending a revision of the Panama Canal Treaty, resumed relations briefly a few days later (Jan. 14) and then broke them again (Jan. 17) . . . Panama proclaimed her intention of taking the dispute to the OAS despite U.S. efforts to prevent it.

The government controlled press of Ghana proclaimed (Jan. 8) total war on capitalism . . . A leftist uprising ousted the pro-western Arab government of Zanzibar off the east coast of Africa . . . sympathetic uprisings in Kenya, Tanganyika and Uganda were suppressed by British troops . . . The new Zanzibar government ousted the U.S. consul at the point of a bayonet.

Recognition of Red China was announced by the French government and when France exchanged ministers with the Reds, the Nationalist Chinese on Formosa severed diplomatic relations with France . . . **President de Gaulle** announced that France favored the neutralization of the Indochina region of South East Asia, including South Viet Nam. He urged that Red China be made a party to the neutralization . . . **President Johnson** sent Attorney General Robert F. Kennedy to President Sukarno of Indonesia to persuade him to call off his attacks on the new state of Malaysia. After appearing to yield to Kennedy's persuasion, Sukarno reaffirmed his hostility to Malaysia following Kennedy's departure.

Premier Fidel Castro made an official visit to the Soviet Union (Jan. 14).

Britain asked U.S., France, Italy and West Germany to help preserve peace in Cyprus (Jan. 26) and three days later Britain and the U.S. jointly proposed that a multi-national force of 10,000 men undertake the peace-keeping task.

SPORTS

In New Year's Day football games Texas beat Navy in the Cotton Bowl 28-6, Alabama beat Mississippi in the Sugar Bowl 12-7, Nebraska edged Auburn in the Orange Bowl and Illinois defeated Washington 17-7 in the Rose Bowl . . . **The Chicago Bears** took the National Football League championship from the favored New York Giants by a score of 14-10 . . . Columbia Broadcasting System paid $28.2 million for the rights to televise National Football League Games in 1964 and 1965, more than three times the price of $9.3 million for television rights covering the years 1962 and 1963.

OBITUARIES

Jack Teagarden, 58, trombone player, one of the greats of jazz. (Jan. 15)

Joseph Schildkraut, 68, stage and screen star, winner of two Academy awards. (Jan. 21)

Marc Blitzstein, 58, composer for the English adaptation of The Threepenny Opera (Mack the Knife) which ran for six years off-Broadway in New York. (Jan. 21)

Alan Ladd, 50, who starred as a tough guy in more than 150 movies. (Jan. 29)

1/29/64— Seven years, three months and 25 days after Sputnik I, America caught up to, and passed, Soviet Union in space race, launching 1.5-million-pound-thrust Saturn I rocket which placed world's heaviest satellite (10 tons) into orbit. Only catch in blast-off was when sea gull got into cameraman's way (right).

NATIONAL NEWS

1/4/64— Under light rain, with 200 jeering, but otherwise calm students looking on, 31-year-old Harold Franklin enrolled in Auburn University graduate school, becoming first Negro to do so.

1/8/64— President less than six weeks, Lyndon B. Johnson delivered his first State of the Union message, announcing budget of $97.9 billion to joint session of Congress. Hailed as a classic political doctrine, Johnson's program proposed Federal measures to combat poverty, predicted sharp deficit spending.

1/10/64— Mrs. John F. Kennedy greets crowd which gathered outside old State Department Building when she paid first visit there to thank volunteer workers helping her answer thousands of letters she has received. Congress appropriated $50,000 for the purpose. Secret Service agent accompanied former First Lady.

1/14/64— Smoke pours from the wreckage of small plane which slammed into empty classroom at Oklahoma Baptist University's Shawnee Hall. Pilot — Robert Lawson, 43, of Inola, Okla. — was killed, but 300 students in building at time of accident were not hurt.

1/17/64— Little girl with big spirit holds up five fingers when President Johnson asked her age during White House visit. She's Mary Lou Graves, 1964 March of Dimes poster girl, who was on 10,000-mile national tour.

1/17/64 — Astronaut John H. Glenn Jr., and his wife Annie flash back-to-earth smiles in Columbus, O., as he announces intention to seek Democratic nomination for Senator from Ohio. The 42-year-old Marine Corps officer, first American to orbit the earth, said he felt he would be too old by the time Project Apollo would be ready to place man on moon. His resignation from program hampered National Space Agency.

1/20/64— Deaths of 31 "skid row" derelicts, caused by drinking "canned heat," led to arrest of variety store owner Max Feinberg in Philadelphia. Feinberg allegedly sold sterno to victims with knowledge that they planned to drink it. Death toll included one woman.

1/16/64— Surfacing from hatch of nuclear submarine USS Sea Wolf at Norfolk, Va., is Italian President Antonio Segni, here on tour.

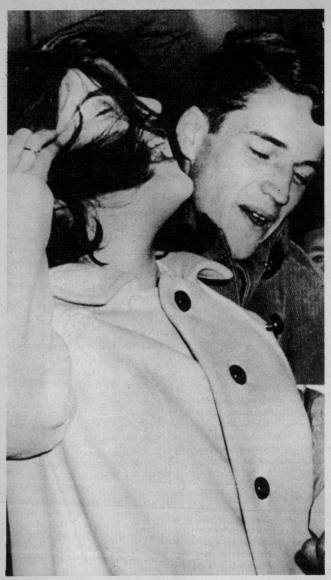

1/25/64 — Luci Baines Johnson receives warm but windy reception at Maiden Rock, Wisconsin, where escort Jack Olson took her to meet his parents.

1/25/64— Fiery blast-off from Vandenberg Air Force Base, Calif., marks first joint U.S.-Russia venture in space as Echo II flares into orbit. A tissue-thin aluminum balloon, it was largest satellite ever launched, opening to 135-foot diameter after being put into orbit by Thor-Agena B rocket. To be used for communication experiments, it should last three years.

1/26/64— Negro girl is comforted by companions after she was injured in scuffle outside Atlanta, Ga., restaurant in civil rights demonstration. Unrest flared for whole week as Negroes attempted to integrate downtown eating places. One restaurant chain relented, but others resisted. Violence was minimal but arrests ran over 300.

1/27/64— Old friend becomes new White House resident as Warrie Lynn Smith (right) is greeted by Lynda Bird and Mrs. Johnson. Girls were classmates at Texas U. and plan to enter George Washington U.

1/28/64— First shipment of U.S. wheat, bound for Russia, is loaded aboard American-owned ship in Norfolk, Va. Grain is part of $78.5 million cash deal which hinged on use of American ships for transport.

1/27/64— National report showed five Americans every two hours, one every 24 minutes, commit suicide, while another 35 try but fail. Three out of four who take their own lives are men, while West Coast (California, Nevada, Utah and Montana) has highest incident of suicide.

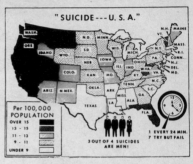

"SUICIDE --- U. S. A."

Per 100,000 POPULATION
OVER 15
13 - 15
11 - 13
9 - 11
UNDER 9

3 OUT OF 4 SUICIDES ARE MEN!

1 EVERY 24 MIN.
7 TRY BUT FAIL

1/28/64— Out of hiding after living in secret location for two months under protective custody of the Secret Service, Mrs. Marina Oswald, wife of accused presidential assassin Lee Harvey Oswald, holds her youngest daughter Rachel during television interview in Dallas. It was first public appearance for Russian-born Mrs. Oswald since the death of her husband.

1/30/64— Relief cuts by state of Illinois prompted protest by Negro mothers and children in Chicago, asking for jobs, surplus food for families on relief (top photo). In Cleveland, lone Negro became involved in fight with a white man, was set upon by an angry mob (bottom photo). Police arrived as picture was taken, stopped fight.

NATIONAL NEWS-END

CANAL ZONE

1/9/64— Joyous, flag-waving American students pour from Balboa High School in Panama Canal Zone for demonstration which directly led to severe diplomatic crisis.

INTERNATIONAL NEWS

1/9/64— Raising of American flag led to clash between American, Panamanian students. Canal Zone police intervened, were forced to fire to restore order.

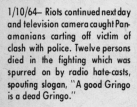

1/10/64— Riots continued next day and television camera caught Panamanians carting off victim of clash with police. Twelve persons died in the fighting which was spurred on by radio hate-casts, spouting slogan, "A good Gringo is a dead Gringo."

1/12/64— Diplomatic relations with U.S. broken, Panama President Roberto Chiari and Vice President Sergio Gonzales Ruiz (right) reflected grimness of situation as they led throng of 40,000 at funeral for riot victims. They demanded new Canal Zone treaty be negotiated. Two days later U.S. troopships arrived in Colon harbor.

1/17/64— As situation grew more tense, U.S. Embassy had orders to evacuate Panama. Embassy officials and their dependents registered at theater in Canal Zone.

1/28/64— While Inter-American Peace Commission sought to mediate dispute, crowd of some 7,000 gathered for field Mass at Cathedral Plaza in Panama City to pray for Panamanian leaders assigned to conduct negotiations with U.S.

1/19/64— Nothing settled, but tension still high, 17-year-old James Jenkins, one of American boys involved in crisis-triggering flag-raising incident, prepares to leave Panama for U.S. A resident in the Canal Zone for 15 years, Jenkins said he had done nothing to "be ashamed of" and had no regrets. Still, he left voluntarily in effort to ease tension. By then, however, dispute had gone far beyond the flying of flags. First OAS mediation attempts failed as Panama insisted that 1903 treaty giving U.S. rights "in perpetuity" over the Canal be re-negotiated, while Washington would promise only to discuss "areas of conflict."

1/5/64— Pope Paul VI (right) and Patriarch Athenagoras I embrace in Jerusalem at historic meeting, the first between heads of Roman Catholic and Eastern Orthodox churches in five centuries. They discussed ending great schism in Christianity that occurred 900 years ago.

1/8/64— Railroad tank cars holding 5,500 tons of crude oil, ticketed for Russia, wait to roll in Vienna, Austria. Oil represented final Austrian payment under terms of reparation treaty signed with Soviet Union in 1955. Originally obligated to pay 10-million tons, Austria earned 3.5-million ton reduction through negotiations conducted by former Chancellor Julius Raab.

1/10/64— British Royal Air Force detachment places itself and its vehicles between Greek and Turkish forces on Cyprus in effort to halt fighting.

1/10/64— Red Chinese Premier Chou En-Lai (left) is greeted by ideological ally, Albanian Communist Party leader Enver Hoxha in Albania where Chou delivered speech re-emphasizing China's committment to "revolution" as means of furthering Communism; thus widening split with Soviet Union.

1/10/64— Buddhist leaders gather in Saigon for first time since downfall of Diem government to determine future policies. Portraits of Buddhist martyrs, whose deaths triggered opposition to Nhu regime, loom in background.

1/12/64— Month-old nation of Zanzibar cringed under bloody coup d'etat engineered by Shiekh Abeid Marume (left), a Communist, who appointed himself Premier and Shiekh Abdul Rahman Babu (second from left) as Defense Minister. Ousted were Prime Minister Mohammed Shamte (second from right) and Sultan Jamshid Bin Abdullah Bin Khalifa (far right). Fighting forces were led by Cuban-trained John Okello (center below), a 27-year-old Bantu tribesman. New government established Swahili as official language, replacing English.

1/16/64— British Army air dispatcher (foreground) watches a one-ton air-drop of supplies to jungle outpost, manned by Malaysian and British security forces along the Indonesian border on the island of Borneo.

1/12/64 — Thirteen-nation Arab League conference in Cairo ends two-year feud between King Hussein of Jordan (right) and Egyptian President Nasser.

1/20/64— Mutinous troops of Tanganyika Rifles are marched off at gunpoint by British Royal Marine Commandos, sent in to end uprising after appeal by Tanganyikan government. Poor pay prompted Rilfes, led by Sandhurst-trained African (insert), to seize their British officers.

1/24/64— Russia's most modern surface vessel, a guided-missile "Kynda" class destroyer, is revealed in photo release by West German Navy. Ship is capable of 38 knots, has two four-tube rocket launchers. Missiles' range is 300 to 400 miles, carry nuclear warheads.

1/28/64— Unarmed American T39 jet training plane was shot down over East Germany, killing (left to right) Capt. John Lorraine of Florida, Lt. Col. Gerald Hannaford of Texas, and Capt. Donald Millard of Calif. "A shocking, senseless act," said Sec. of State Dean Rusk.

1/30/64— Maj. Gen. Nguyen Khanh (insert, left) staged bloodless coup in Saigon, Viet Nam, ousting Maj. Gen. Dhuong Van Minh (insert, right). Khanh, American - trained, surrounds junta headquarters with tanks. He placed Minh under house arrest. Soldier in full-battle dress guards deposed leader's residence.

INTERNATIONAL NEWS-END

1/27/64— French actress Brigitte Bardot and Moroccan-born, used-car salesman, Bob Zaguri, were snapped in unguarded moments (above, top photo next page) by Swedish yachtsman. When published later, photos made Brigitte boil.

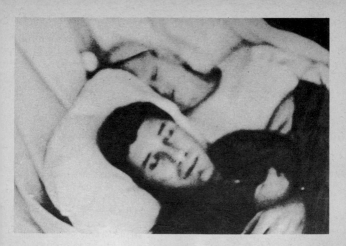

1/19/64— Veteran race driver Joe Weatherly skidded out of control during Riverside (Cal.) 500-mile stock car race, hit retaining wall on Turn 6 and died. Attendants lift his body from crumpled wreckage.

1/15/64— "Say Hey Kid" Willie Mays says "yea" to his 1964 contract with San Francisco Giants. Pact called for salary of $105,000, highest sum ever paid a major-league baseball player.

1/9/64— Mandy Rice-Davies, key, and spree figure in Britain's "Profumo scandal," makes debut as nightclub singer in "Eve" bar in Munich. Her fee? $200 a night.

1/24/64— American Hayes Jones (dark jersey) flashes to new world's indoor record of 5.9 seconds for 50-yard high hurdles at Maple Leaf Garden in Toronto. Jones led all the way, clipping 1/10 of a second off mark, scored his 50th win in a row.

1/29/64— Olympic flame burns brightly as Winter Games open in Innsbruck, Austria. Austrian Egon Zimmerman, at left, barrelled through snow flurries to win men's downhill race, as expected. American men failed to win a skiing event, but did take second and third in slalom, our best showing ever. In pairs figure skating (top photo, next page), Russian pair (center) won gold medal; West German couple (left) were second with Canadians Debbi Wilkes and Guy Revell finishing third.

1/31/64— U. S. speed skater Janice Smith is carried off ice by Olympic officials after she fell crossing finish line in 1,500-meter race. She was not badly hurt.

1/20064— Baseball's man of the year, Los Angeles Dodger pitcher Sandy Koufax, becomes Professional Athlete of the Year, an honor of no small value, since with it goes a $10,000 jewel-studded Hickok Belt awarded at dinner in Rochester. Sandy won 25 games, stopped Yanks in World Series.

1/27/64— Elizabeth Taylor and Richard Burton on way to Hollywood press conference after return from Mexico, where he was making a film. Couple plans to fly to Toronto where Burton will begin working in a stage production of Hamlet, which will eventually open in New York City.

1/7/64— Spring fashions take big plunge, both in front and in back, at show in New York. Designer Ceil Chapman gave foot-deep neckline on black crepe (left), while Luis Estevaz' triangle shoulder gave similar appearance to back of short gown (right).

1/26/64— Heavyweight champion Sonny Liston (left) arrives in Miami for title fight with Cassius Clay, who was there to greet him (right).

1/20/64— Two movie queens of a reign or two apart – Italian actress Claudia Cardinale and the beautiful Rita Hayworth – appear in scene for film they are making in Madrid. They are cast as mother and daughter.

1/21/64— Unidentified woman (L) wields stick while another kneels with brick on head and in each hand as she demonstrates for judge in Leon, Mexico, incredible mistreatment of prisoners in "white slave" concentration camp. The court held two sisters and five accomplices on charges of homicide stemming from deaths of 11 persons whose bodies were found in the camp.

1/29/64— French-Algerian refugee couple arrive with smiles and a baby carriage in Buenos Aires, Argentina. They are part of immigrant group, sponsored by French government, which will form a farming cooperative in the Argentine.

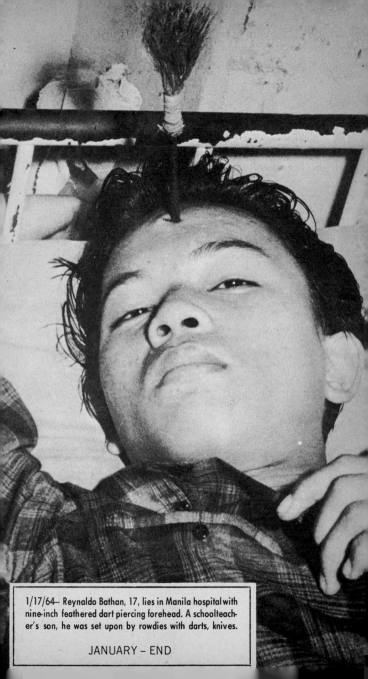

1/17/64— Reynaldo Bathan, 17, lies in Manila hospital with nine-inch feathered dart piercing forehead. A schoolteacher's son, he was set upon by rowdies with darts, knives.

JANUARY – END

SUMMARY - FEBRUARY 1964

NATIONAL

U.S. spacecraft Ranger VI completed (Feb. 2) its 66-hour journey to the moon on schedule but failed to televise pictures back to earth as planned because of an unexplained failure in the equipment.

Dr. Eric Goldman of Princeton University was appointed (Feb. 3) special consultant to President Lyndon B. Johnson "to channel the nation's best thinking into the White House......" **Former St. Louis Cardinal baseball star**, Stan Musial, was named (Feb. 14) to head a national physical fitness program...... **Sargent Shriver**, head of the Peace Corps and brother-in-law of the late President John F. Kennedy, was chosen (Feb. 7) by President Johnson to direct "the war against poverty in the U.S.".......**Roger Stevens**, New York real estate tycoon and theatrical producer, appointed director of the Johnson administration's cultural program.

Boycott of New York City schools in protest against segregation cut city-wide attendance by 460,000 students (Feb. 3)...... **Sweeping civil rights bill passed** (Feb. 10) by U.S. House of Representatives by a vote of 290-130. Bill makes it a **violation of Federal law to discriminate against Negroes in such public facilities as hotels, motels and restaurants and to interfere with their right to vote**...... In Jackson, Mississippi, a jury was unable (Feb. 7) to reach a verdict in the trial of **Byron De La Beckwith** for the murder of Negro civil rights executive Medgar Evers. Jury was reported to favor acquittal 7-5.

Ban against smoking in hotel and motel rooms was voted (Feb. 4) by New York's City Council. Hotel industry said the ban would be unenforceable...... **England's "Beatles"**, rock and roll singing group, arrived for their first visit to U.S. (Feb. 7) and met with the expected hysterical reception from teen-age packs of girls...... New York's **Metropolitan Opera** banned standees because of threats to stars but rescinded ban within 24 hours when pro-standee groups picketed the opera house...... 17 unpublished songs by George Gershwin, noted popular composer of the Twenties, were released for publication (Feb. 16)...... It was reported (Feb. 21) that noted author **Ernest Hemingway** left a fortune of nearly $1.5 million in "blue chip" securities.

International Longshoremen's Association refused to load wheat ships destined for Soviet Union charging violation of agreement to ship multi-million dollar wheat purchase by Reds in ships flying American flags (Feb. 16). After intervention by President Johnson, ILA cancelled boycott (Feb. 25) on promise to ship at least 50 per cent of wheat in American flag ships.

U.S. Supreme Court ruled, 6-3, that election districts for U.S. House of Representatives must be roughly equal in population (Feb. 17)......Same day, Court set aside deportation order against **Frank Costello**, alleged former head of Mafia.

Robert G. Baker, former Secretary to the Democratic Senate Majority, was charged before a Senate Rules Committee investigating committee with having pledged stock he did not own as security for a bank loan.

$11.5 billion tax cut bill was signed (Feb. 26) by President Johnson. Bill, which does not become fully effective until 1965, cuts individual taxes by an average of 19 per cent, corporate taxes by $2.4 billion.

Trial of Jack Ruby, Dallas, Tex. nightspot manager, for murder of Lee Harvey Oswald, alleged assassin of President Kennedy, opened (Feb. 8) in Dallas. By Feb. 29, selection of a jury had not yet been completed.

It was reported (Feb. 24) that accidents in the U.S. took **100,500** lives in 1963.

President Johnson completed 100 days as President (Feb. 29). The same day he announced the secret development of a supersonic jet plane, the A-11, capable of traveling 2,000 miles per hour at an altitude of 70,000 feet. Produced by Lockheed Aircraft Corporation, plane was said to be in production.

INTERNATIONAL

President Johnson rejected (Feb. 1) "for the present" a negotiated peace in Viet Nam proposed by President de Gaulle...... Britain's Prime Minister, Sir Alec Douglas-Home, backed the U.S. policy in Viet Nam at a meeting (Feb. 12) with President Johnson in Washington. **The British chief executive refused at the same meeting to promise an end to Britain's trade with Cuba and failed to get U.S. official support for Britain's siding with Malaysia in her conflict with Indonesia.**

A **United Nations peace force** for Cyprus under the control of the Security Council was approved in principle (Feb. 4) by Greece and Turkey but rejected by the government of Cyprus...... Britain called (Feb. 15) for an emergency meeting of the U.N. Security Council to consider a Turkish threat to invade Cyprus.

Ghana became a one-party state (Feb. 2) following a national referendum. President Kwame Nkrumah accused the U.S. of complicity in a plot to assassinate him.

Cuba cut off the water supply of the U.S. Navy base in Guantanamo (Feb. 6) in retaliation for the seizure of four Cuban fishing boats found trespassing in U.S. waters off the coast of Florida. Senator Barry Goldwater urged the U.S. Government to send a detachment of marines into Cuba to turn the water on...... **The Organization of American States (OAS)** appointed (Feb. 6) a 17-nation committee to mediate the dispute between the U.S. and Panama over revision of the Panama Canal Treaty between the two countries...... **Venezuela's charge of aggression** against Cuba was upheld (Feb. 24) by the OAS and the member nations agreed to have their foreign ministers meet to consider the imposition of sanctions against the government of Fidel Castro.

A **high official** of the Soviet Russian secret police, Yuri Ivanovich Nossenko defected to the west (Feb. 10) while serving as a delegate to East-West disarmament talks in Geneva.

Zanzibar severed dimplomatic relations (Feb. 19) with the U.S. and Britain over their failure to recognize the leftist government which seized power a month earlier. Four days later both the U.S. and Britain granted recognition...... President Leon Mbu of Gabon, former French colony in Africa, was ousted in a military coup (Feb. 18) and immediately restored to power by French troops.

SPORTS

Track star Wendell Motley of Yale broke the world's indoor record for 440 yards at the 75th running of the Boston A.A. Games (Feb. 1) with a mark of 48 seconds. Old record, established in 1942, was 48.2 seconds.

The Soviet Union won its third straight victory in the Winter Olympics at Innsbruck, Austria, mainly with the help of ice-skating speedster Lidia Skoblikova who picked up four gold medals to add to the two she won in 1960.

Tom O'Hara of Loyola University in Chicago clipped a full two seconds off the world's indoor mile track record of 3 minutes 58.6 seconds in the New York Athletic Club Games at Madison Square Garden (Feb. 13).

Chuck McKinley defeated Dennis Ralston (Feb. 24) in the finals of the U.S. Indoor Tennis Championships in five sets.

Cassius Marcellus Clay Jr., an eight-to-one underdog, scored a technical knockout (Feb. 25) in the seventh round to take the world's heavyweight boxing title from Charles (Sonny) Liston at Miami Beach.

OBITUARIES

Clarence Buddington Kelland, 82, popular writer and creator of such famous characters as Scattergood Baines, Mark Tidd and Mr. Deeds ("Mr. Deeds Goes to Washington"). (Feb. 18)

Grace Metalious, 39, author of the notorious novel, "Peyton Place". (Feb. 29)

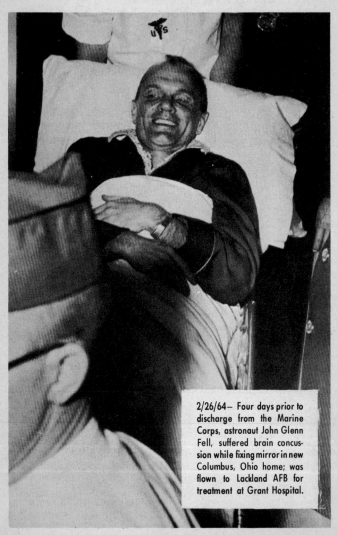

2/26/64— Four days prior to discharge from the Marine Corps, astronaut John Glenn Fell, suffered brain concussion while fixing mirror in new Columbus, Ohio home; was flown to Lackland AFB for treatment at Grant Hospital.

2/6/64— President Johnson deftly wards off light nudge by policeman's horse on visit to New York. Despite rain, LBJ greeted crowds.

NATIONAL NEWS

INVESTIGATION OF PRESIDENT KENNEDY'S ASSASSINATION

2/3/64— Mrs. Marina Oswald arrives in Washington to testify before seven-man Warren Commission.

2/17/64— Mrs. Marguerite Oswald, mother of accused assassin, tells press in New York son was CIA agent.

2/20/64— Assassin's brother, Robert Oswald, was "very cooperative witness" before the Commission.

2/27/64— Houston paper said James Martin, adviser to Oswald's wife, knew of plot to kill former VP Nixon.

2/3/64— Outdoor rally climaxes anti-segregation boycott of New York public schools. The one-day boycott was more successful than even its leaders predicted; one-third of city's million students stayed home.

2/3/64— Wally Schirra (right foreground), one of seven original astronauts and an orbital flight veteran, greets 14 new astronauts, all jet pilots, as they began training in Texas for moon flight within next ten years.

2/4/64— Threatened integration by Negro students of Macon County High School in Nostasulga, Ala., brings state troopers to scene; one lone student leaves classes at his father's insistence. Negro students didn't show up until next day, but were then turned away by town mayor. Free lance photographer on school bus was beaten.

2/5/64— Famed Oklahoma University football coach Bud Wilkinson announces his candidacy for Republican nomination for U. S. Senator in Oklahoma City. He headed JFK's fitness program.

2/6/64— Honor guard carries flag-draped caskets of three Air Force officers killed when their unarmed jet trainer was shot down by Soviets over East Germany last month. Plane transporting bodies arrived at Andrews Air Force Base.

TRIAL OF BYRON DE LA BECKWITH

2/6/64 — All-white, male jury leaves Jackson, Miss., courthouse to decide fate of Bryon De La Beckwith, accused killer of Negro Medgar Evers.

2/7/64 — Mrs. De La Beckwith (left) appears relieved after mistrial was declared when jury, after 22 hours, split 7-5 for acquittal. In Little Rock, Ark., Mrs. Evers tells NAACP meeting that her husband, who was slain from ambush, gave his life "gladly" for Negro cause.

2/10/64 — Two oft-mentioned but publicly reluctant candidates for GOP's presidential nomination, Michigan Governor George Romney (left) and Pennsylvania Governor William Scranton, breakfast in Detroit.

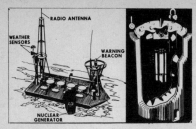

2/6/64 — Navy announced it has placed first atomic-powered NOMAD weather station on duty in Gulf of Mexico, 350 miles south of New Orleans. Fully automatic, it will radio weather information every hour.

2/9/64— Dawn explosion blasts 32 freight cars of Florida East Coast Railway off track in Miami. Officials of strike-bound line said saboteurs set blast. Week later dynamite bomb derailed freight train in New Smyrna Beach. Similar explosion occurred two weeks later in St. Augustine.

SINATRA, JR KIDNAP CASE

2/10/64— Three defendants in Frank Sinatra Jr., kidnaping arrive for start of trial in Los Angeles. They are (left to right) Joseph Amsler, 23, Barry Keenan, 23 and John Irwin, 42. Trumpeter John Foss (bottom photo) was key state witness. He shared room with young Sinatra at Lake Tahoe lodge; identified Keenan as first man to enter their room on night of the abduction.

2/13/64 — Young Sinatra exits briskly from courthouse (opposite page) after testifying he took kidnapers' advice, "played it cool," rather than trying to escape. Frank Sr., (left) gave details on negotiations with kidnapers, while singer Dean Torrance (with glasses, and partner Jan Barry) contradicted himself on stand, first denying then admitting he knew of crime in advance, received part of the $240,000 ransom.

2/10/64— Ohio State coed Marjorie Cocoziello, 19, was arrested for jaywalking in Columbus, jailed 1-1/2 hours; student reaction on next page.

2/12/64— Over 5,000 OSU students stopped traffic in protest over jaywalking arrest.

2/12/64— Face of the John F. Kennedy half-dollar — minting of the coin started today.

2/12/64— Mrs. Henry Ford II, in Sun Valley with daughters Anne (left) and Charlotte, was granted divorce (settlement reportedly came to $16 million), ending 23-year marriage to automobile magnate, who plans to marry 34-year-old Italian divorcee, Christina Austin (below, right).

2/18/64— Frank Rodriguez, 18 (left), New York Boys' Club's "boy of the year" for 1963 was shot and killed by probationary patrolman in street brawl. His wife Anna, holding 11-month-old son, is pregnant.

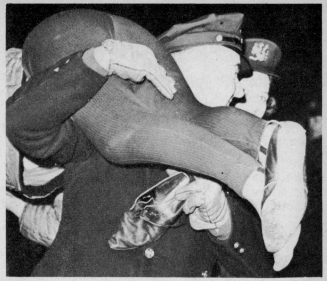

2/21/64— One of six girls who fainted when Beatle fans gave their shaggy idols riotous sendoff from JFK Airport is carried off by police.

2/21/64— Discount house's 99-cent bargain sale created near riot in Pittsburgh. Many customers waited in line all night, then stormed doors, broke windows to get in. Police were called to hold back the mob.

2/25/64 — Arthur J. Holland, mayor of Trenton, N. J., greets group of young neighbors. He bought 100-year-old, 14-room colonial house in rundown, inter-racial area of the city. Standing on stoop is his wife Cynthia, who is holding their 10-month-old daughter.

BOBBY BAKER

2/25/64 — Former Senate aide Bobby Baker (left above with attorney Edward Bennett Williams) makes long-awaited appearance before the Senate Rules Committee, concerning his far-flung business dealings. Previous testimony indicated Baker was involved in meat export deal, insurance kickbacks, vending machine firm, but he refused either to testify or turn over his records. Girl Friday Carole Tyler (right) also refused to answer questions.

★

2/26/64— Former St. Louis Cardinal baseball great Stan Musial (right) is congratulated by President Johnson after being sworn in as President's Special Consultant on Physical Fitness.

2/27/64 — From rostrum, President Johnson pushes button, sets off explosion (right) to start construction of Cross Florida Barge Canal at Palatka, Fla. Canal will link Atlantic Ocean with the Gulf of Mexico when completed.

2/17/64 — Prospective jurors in Jack Ruby murder trial wait examination in Dallas courthouse. More than 900 were summoned for possible duty in the case of man who shot accused presidential assassin, Lee Harvey Oswald last November.

2/28/64— Carl T. Rowan, his wife and two boys pose with President Johnson after Rowan was sworn in as Director of U.S. Information Agency in Washington. Rowan, a Negro and former Minneapolis newsman, succeeds Edward R. Murrow.

NATIONAL NEWS-END

TROUBLE IN CUBA

2/2/64— Cuban fisherman, poaching in U.S. waters, touched off Guantanamo water crisis. Coast Guard seized four boats (top photo), brought them to Key West with all hands (36) aboard. Four days later Castro retaliated, shutting off fresh water to Guantanamo Naval Base, forcing Navy to rely on reserve supply of 15 million gallons stored in tanks on base (second from top). Fishermen were released from custody on same day in Key West (third from top), but tension was still high. Armed Cuban guards ringed base (opposite page), watched American children play on beach. Meanwhile U.S. sent tanker "Tallulah" which arrived Feb. 16 (above).

2/17/64— After decision to make Guantanamo self-sufficient — by constructing
$4,000,000 salt-water conversion plant — Navy severed Castro's pipeline. U. S.
also decided against employing Cubans, let 500 go immediately; planned to with-
draw dependents thru normal rotation.

2/4/64— Emerson Player of Denver, Colo., a Negro U.S. Embassy official in Accra, Ghana, braved anti-American mob to hoist Stars and Stripes after it had been torn down.

CYPRUS

2/6/64— Dead Greek Cypriot is pulled to cover (below) after ambush by Turks in north of Cyprus. Continued violence on island, due to Turkish minority's fears of Greek majority (see map), caused U.S. to begin evacuating American women and children.

WHERE TURKS LIVE

WHERE GREEKS LIVE

TOWNS WITH TURKISH MINORITIES

2/6/64— Bitter fighting in Turkish village of Ayios Sozemenos on Cyprus took heavy toll. Turkish Cypriot (left) covers body of his 12-year-old brother, slain during gun battle.

2/27/64— Turkish Ambassador to U.S. (left) and Greek Ambassador to U.N. arrive for Security Council session. Cyprus Foreign Minister charged Turkey threatens world peace. Turks said they sought only "peace and stability" on island.

2/7/64— Three U.S. Winter Olympic athletes, with Austrian police between them, sit in Innsbruck court, charged with brawling with police. Americans claimed authorities gave them brutal beatings.

2/9/64— Royal sweethearts, Princess Irene, 24, of The Netherlands, and Prince Hugo Carlos de Bourbon Parma, Carlist pretender to throne of Spain, stroll in Palace Garden in Amsterdam. They are engaged to be married, but there is much opposition to match in Holland.

AFRICA

2/4/64— Soviet security agent Yuri Nossenko at Geneva disarmament talks, just before defecting to West. He had access to top secrets.

2/7/64— Newsmap reveals new face of Africa as "wind of change" continues to sweep continent. Great majority of new African nations did not achieve independence till after WW II.

2/12/64— Covered with oil, survivors of Australia's worst peacetime sea disaster sit aboard rescue boat. Their ship, the Australian destroyer "Voyager," was sunk when rammed by aircraft carrier "Melbourne." Total of 82 were still missing.

2/17/64— U.S. Air Force "spotter" plane flies cover for South Viet Nam truck convoy, against possible ambush by Communist Viet Cong. Red terrorist tactics have increased security precautions.

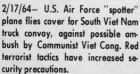

2/13/64— Six days before he was to go on trial for supervising Nazis' so-called "mercy killing" of 100,000 Germans, Dr. Werner Heyde, 61, hanged himself in jail cell in Limburg. Day before, another defendant leaped nine floors to his death. Jailed four years ago, Heyde had changed his identity after World War II, had flourishing practice in northern Germany, even collected some $75,000 in fees as expert medical witness in state courts. During war, he directed Hitler's program to purify Aryan race by killing mental defectives. Only one defendant, Dr. Hans Hefelmann, was alive to face trial.

2/19/64— Meriel Douglas-Home, daughter of British Prime Minister, poses with her fiance, Adrian Darby, in London. He is a teacher.

2/24/64— Small life raft pushes off from floundering British freighter "Ambassador" in North Atlantic. Coast Guard rescued survivors.

2/19/64 – Italian President Antonio Segni (at left) and French President Charles de Gaulle ride in open sedan following Segni's arrival in Paris for discussions concerning increased European cooperation, nuclear policy and relations with United States.

2/23/64 – Communist China's first diplomatic envoy to France, Sung Chi-Kuang, arrives in Paris from Switzerland. France broke solid Western front by recognizing Red Chinese, hinted recognition would be withdrawn from Nationalists. Chiang Kai-shek countered by breaking off relations with Paris. His envoys had not cleared embassy by Chi-Kuang's arrival; he stayed at a hotel.

2/26/64 – Tanganyikan President Julius Nyerere addresses loyalty rally in Dar Es Salaam. It was his first public appearance since recent revolt of Tanganyika Rifles. In speech, Nyerere criticized government workers for neglecting their jobs.

2/27/64 – Former New York socialite Hope Cooke, now Queen Hope Namgyal of tiny Himalayan kingdom of Sikkim, fondles her new son in Calcutta hospital. King has three other children by previous marriage. Pre-marital agreement forbids new son from ever reigning.

2/26/64 – Asian refugees from Zanzibar are rowed ashore in Tanganyika after safe passage on ship "Jumuri". More than 4,000 Asians have fled island since recent African-led revolt.

2/27/64 – New President of People's Republic of Zanzibar, Abeid Amani Karume (at left) links hands with Field Marshal John Okello who led revolt. U.S. and Britain recognized leftist group, hoping it would move into neutral camp rather than Communist orbit.

INTERNATIONAL NEWS-END

ENTERTAINMENT, SPORTS & THE ARTS

WINTER OLYMPICS

2/2/64 – Russia's Lidia Skoblikova (right) is congratulated by friend after winning women's 3,000-meter speed-skating event in Winter Olympics. It was Miss Skoblikova's fourth gold medal, a record.

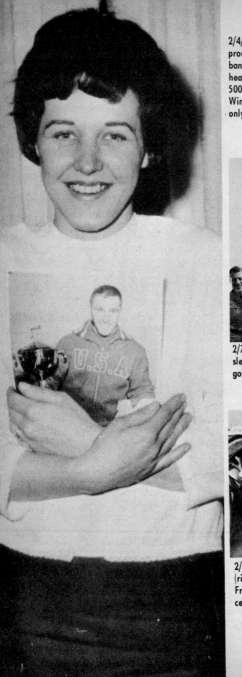

2/4/64— Mrs. Terry McDermott proudly hugs portrait of her husband in Essexville, Mich., after hearing of his victory in men's 500-meter speed-skating event in Winter Olympics. It was U.S.'s only gold medal.

2/7/64— Canada's four-man bobsled team rejoices after winning gold medal, nation's first at Games.

2/3/64— America's Jean Saubert (right) was second in giant slalom. France's Goitschell sisters (left and center) finished 1-3.

2/5/64— America's two-man toboggan team of Ronnie Walters and Jim Higgins careens over edge of run at Innsbruck. Neither was badly hurt, but U.S. pride took beating as Russia dominated Winter Games.

2/2/64— Villanova's two-mile relay team (Tom Sullivan, Noel Carroll, Al Adams, Vic Zwolak) set world indoor record in Boston.

2/12/64— It shouldn't happen to a dog, though it does to sheep, but here's how the lovable lads from Liverpool, alias The Beatles, look like with crew cuts. For the record, and in case you can't tell, they are (left to right) Ringo, George, John and Paul.

2/7/64— Bing Crosby and 5-year-old son Harry giggle over catch made by the youngster at Huck Finn Fishing Pond at San Francisco Sports and Boat Show. Now, if he can only sing!

2/13/64 — Tom O'Hara runs record indoor mile in 3:56.6

2/15/64 — Carlos Ortiz (left) retains 136 pound title against Flash Elorde in Manila.

2/19/64— Actor Peter Sellers and new Swedish bride Britt Eklund in England.

2/23/64— World's first 17-foot pole vaulter John Pennel receives top amateur athlete honor, James E. Sullivan Award in NY.

2/25/64— Injured shoulder forces Sonny Liston to give up heavyweight title to Cassius Clay after sixth round in Miami. Result was shock.

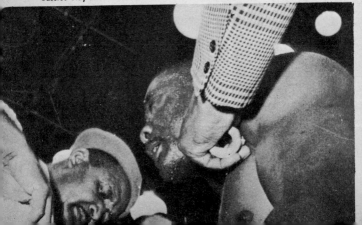

2/22/64– Florida A & M's Bob Hayes sets world record of 5.9 seconds for 60-yard dash in AAU Indoor championships

2/26/64— Security guard ushers in Elizabeth Taylor at dress rehearsal preview of Hamlet in which Richard Burton had title role in Toronto. She almost stole the show.

2/27/64 — Actress Ingrid Bergman, still lovely at 46, relaxes with husband Lars Schmidt, a Swedish industrialist, at St. James, Barbados. Couple recently purchased 12-acre site there, plan to build home.

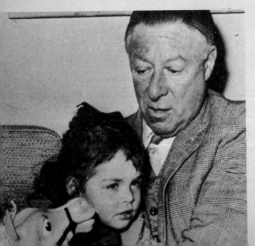

2/29/64- Showman George Jessel and two-year-old daughter Charris greet press at exclusive West Los Angeles Club. Girl is daughter of Joan Tyler, whose paternity suit against Jessel was settled when he agreed to pay $500 monthly. This was his first public appearance with Charris.

2/23/64 — Despite appearances, actress Hayley Mills, 18, is about to place hand prints, not tongue, in cement at Grauman's Chinese Theater. She is first teen-ager so honored.

ENTERTAINMENT
SPORTS & THE ARTS
END

MISCELLANY

2/14/64 — When ban was placed on kissing in girls' dormitory lounges at Indiana University, couples moved out into the cold to say a Valentine's Day goodnight.

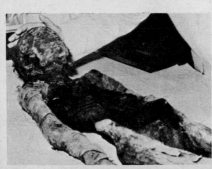

2/12/64—Dead 1,800 years, young girl's body was found on outskirts of Rome. It was so perfectly mummified, authorities first thought it might be that of a recent murder victim.

2/28/64 — Otway Shans of Denver finds foe up in air during 175-pound Golden Gloves bout in Louisville.

2/24/64 — Soviet Cosmonaut Pavel Popovich pops up to sing song during reception in Vienna, Austria.

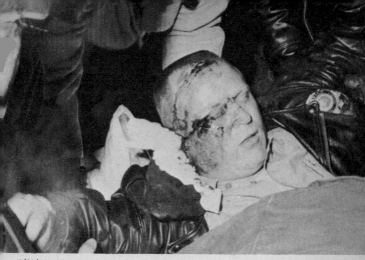

2/24/64 — In struggle with gunman, Carnegie (Pa.) patrolman Richard Hancock had ear bitten off by police K-9 dog. Gunman had held police chief captive three hours before he was surprised by Hancock.

2/28/64 — For first time in Austria, five Roman Catholic nuns, from convent in Mitterbach, are taking skiing lessons. Top photo shows them in their ski togs, bottom photo in their more usual attire.

2/11/64 — The bare facts here are these bare photo mock-ups of a group of Maillol nudes being moved to Tuileries Gardens near the Louvre. They will be used to determine positioning of actual statues, which were too burdensome to carry around. It is all part of campaign to "beautify" Paris.

FEBRUARY – END

SUMMARY - MARCH   1964

NATIONAL

$35 million worth of tickets to the New York World's Fair had been sold (March 2) with the opening still seven weeks away......A decision by a New York judge that New York motorists did not have to accept license plates with a World's Fair advertisement was reversed by a higher state court.

After 16 days of wrangling, a jury was finally chosen (March 3) in the trial of **Jack Ruby** in Dallas, Tex. for the murder of Lee Harvey Oswald, alleged assassin of President John F. Kennedy......The jury found Ruby guilty (March 14) and he was sentenced to die in the electric chair.

John J. McKeithen, democratic candidate for the governorship of Louisiana, defeated a Goldwater republican by the smallest margin in more than 65 years.....Demonstrators belonging to the Congress for Racial Equality (CORE) caused a giant traffic jam in New York City by staging a sitdown on the Triborough Bridge, main link between the island of Manhattan and the crowded boroughs and suburban communities of Long Island ..... **Malcolm X**, no. 2 man in the Black Muslims, Negro nationalist society, and the organization's firebrand, was suspended by Black Muslim leader, Elijah Muhammed for having said after the assassination of President Kennedy, "the chickens are coming home to roost." Malcolm X immediately announced the formation of his own "Black Nationalist Party"......**The U.S. Senate** began (March 12) debating whether to debate the Civil Rights Law which the House of Representatives had already passed......A seven-man bi-racial committee was formed in Jacksonville, Florida, to try to find a means of ending riots which had already lasted two days.

James R. Hoffa, boss of the International Brotherhood of Teamsters, was convicted at Chattanooga (March 4) with three others of tampering with a jury during a previous trial. It was the teamster boss's first conviction in six indictments by the Federal Government. He was sentenced to eight years in jail and a fine of $10,000......**A Federal Judge** refused to dismiss the indictment of Roy Cohn, boy wonder of the legal profession and top aide to the late Senator Joseph McCarthy, because of a mail watch instituted by Federal authorities. The judge called the watch "shocking". **Cohn** had been indicted for conspiracy to commit perjury......**The U.S. Supreme Court**, nullifying (March 9) a $500,000 libel judgment against the New York Times on behalf of officials of the State of Alabama, ruled that a public official cannot sue for libel for criticism of his official acts unless he can prove deliberate malice. The verdict was construed as giving newspapers and other critics almost unlimited right to express disapproval of the records of public officials......**The same day the Court** handed down a ruling to the effect that any unpatented product may be freely copied by anyone ..... **The U.S. Court of Appeals** ruled (March 26) that jail inmates who had been deprived of their right to counsel during their trial should be freed.

The nation was shocked by the murder of 28-year old **Catherine Genovese** in Queens, New York (March 12) while 38 persons in an adjacent apartment building saw and heard the whole thing but failed to call the police or offer help themselves ...... **The Rules Committee of the U.S. Senate** ended its inquiry into the affairs of Robert G. Baker, former Secretary to the Democratic Majority amid widespread criticism by Republicans and the press for failure to probe deeper into Baker's operations.

The U.S. House of Representatives defeated (March 12) by a vote of 222-184 a bill which would have provided pay raises for 1.7 million Federal employees including a raise of $10,000 a year for themselves ,,,,,, **An anti-poverty bill** was sent to Congress by the White House asking $1 billion as an initial budget of which $380 million would be spent during the first year for the training and education of underprivileged youths ...... **President Johnson** requested from Congress the lowest foreign aid appropriation in 16 years, $3.4 billion. In 1963, President Kennedy had asked for $4.9 billion.

Pierre Salinger, holdover press secretary to the White House from the Kennedy administration, resigned (March 19) to seek the Democratic Party's nomination for the U.S. Senate in California. He was succeeded by George Reedy ...... **Cassius Clay**, World's Heavyweight Boxing Champion, failed for the second time to pass the Army's pre-induction tests.

The worst Ohio River flood in 20 years, beginning March 12, had made 30,000 families homeless by March 14 ...... **The most severe earthquake** in modern history to strike the U.S. destroyed an estimated $250 million worth of property in Alaska. Hardest hit area was Anchorage, a city of 60,000 population. Fatalities and injuries were relatively light considering the force of the 'quake although a tidal wave brought death to 12 residents of Crescent City, California. (March 28)

INTERNATIONAL

Senator **J. W. Fulbright**, Democratic Senator from Arkansas and Chairman of the Senate Foreign Relations Committee asked the nation (March 25) to "shed 'myths'" and think daringly about such foreign policy problems as Soviet Russia, communist China, Cuba, Panama and Latin America. He called the Cuba of Fidel Castro a nuisance rather than a menace. Secretary of State Dean Rusk gave the speech the administration's approval but disagreed on Cuba.

Major General Nguyen Khanh, ruler of South Viet Nam, accused the French of plotting to assassinate him. The French called the charge "childish, absurd, ridiculous" ...... Secretary of Defense **Robert S. McNamara**, General Maxwell Taylor, Chairman of the Joint Chiefs of Staff, Central Intelligence Agency chief John A. McCone and William P. Bundy, Assistant Secretary of State for the Far East, flew (March 6) to S. Viet Nam to appraise the deteriorating situation ..... later in the month (March 26), on his return to the U.S., Secretary McNamara rejected "withdrawal, neutralization, peace-at-any-price" as a policy in Viet Nam.

The U.N. Security Council voted (March 4) to set up a peace-keeping force in Cyprus ...... Sakari S. Tuomioja of Finland was appointed (March 24) U.N. Mediator in Cyprus and General Prem Singh of India was named to command U.N. troops.

King Paul of the Hellenes died (March 6), aged 62, and his son, 23-year-old Crown Prince Constantine, succeeded him as King of Greece ...... **President Charles de Gaulle** of France arrived in Mexico (March 16) on a state visit designed to promote French influence in Latin America ...... **Raul Leoni** took office as President of Venezuela (March 11) ...... U.S. Supreme Court ruled that Cuban expropriations of U.S foreign property is legal and cannot be upset by U.S. courts but must be negotiated by diplomacy.

An unarmed U.S. reconnaissance plane was shot down (March 9) over East Germany. Crew of three parachuted to safety. One of crew was injured. After a two-week delay, the Soviet Union released the three crew members.

In London, England, **Charles Cooper**, 46-year-old bachelor and a $29 a week clerk, won $630,375.20 for a 70 cent bet in a football pool ...... **The British Government** voted to pay damages to victims of crimes who are unable to work for at least three weeks ...... One acre of the meadow at Runnymeade, where Magna Charta was signed, was given by the British Government for a memorial to the late President Kennedy.

Brazilian sailors and marines mutinied (March 27) but were granted amnesty when they downed their arms.

King Saud of Saudi Arabia yielded power (March 28) to his half-brother Crown Prince Faisul.

SPORTS

Tom O'Hara of Loyola in Chicago ran the featured mile in the Chicago Daily News Relays (March 6) in 3 minutes 55.4 seconds to break his own world's indoor record by .2 seconds.

Pro-football stars Paul Hornung of the Green Bay Packers and Alexis Karras, suspended a year ago for betting on their own teams were reinstated (March 16)

For the first time since 1938, A U.S. horse, Team Spirit won England's Grand National Steeplechase. The 12-year-old gelding is owned by Jack Goodman of Arizona and Ron Woodward of Indianapolis.

OBITUARIES

Norbert Wiener, 69, M.I.T. mathematician, father of the computer. (March 18)

Brendan Behan, 41, Irish playwright and playboy. (March 20)

Peter Lorre, stage and screen star, noted for villainous roles. (March 23)

3/17/64 — President Johnson outlines American hemispheric policy before Organization of American States in Washington on third anniversary of the Alliance for Progress. On Panama question, he firmly denied U.S. had agreed to re-write 1903 treaty on American rights in Canal Zone, and said there had not been any "genuine meeting of minds" between the two nations. Moving on to Cuba, he reaffirmed policies of the late President Kennedy, said he pledged "full power" of U.S. against Communist aggression in the Americas. He cited examples of Cuba's aggressive designs on her neighbors, and restated that the U.S. will do whatever must be done to protect its own security and that of its allies.

NATIONAL
NEWS

3/22/64 — Young Negro, wearing Student Non-Violent Coordinating Committee button, stages one-man protest at Ku Klux Klan rally in Georgia.

RUBY TRIAL

3/4/64 — Chief defense attorney Melvin Belli based his case on insanity.

3/4/64 — District Attorney Henry Wade directed the prosecution against Ruby.

3/3/64 — Judge J. Frank Wilson presided when Judge Brown became sick.

Max E. Causey   Allen W. McCoy   Mrs. Mildred McCollum   Luther Gene Dickerson   Douglas J. Sowell   R. J. Flechtner, Jr.

Mrs. Gwen L. English   J. G. Holton   James E. Cunningham   J. Wayman Rose   Mrs. Aileen B. Shields   Mrs. Louis Malone

THE JURY

3/14/64 — After two hours, 19 minutes of deliberation, jury found Jack Ruby "guilty of murder with malice and assessed the penalty at death." Verdict touched off noisy, highly-vocal denunciation by defense attorney Belli, who shouted, "This is the biggest kangaroo court disgrace in the history of American law." District Attorney Wade countered: "They pitched their whole case on insanity ... it was as weak a case of psychiatric defense as I've seen." Belli presented medical testimony that Ruby had brain damage, was not responsible for his actions. Prosecution's medical experts disclaimed brain damage theory. Most damaging witness was Dallas policeman, who testified Ruby, after shooting Oswald, said he had thought about it for two days. Defense claimed Judge's charge to jury directed verdict of guilty. And so the jury voted, unanimously.

TRIAL SIDELIGHT

3/6/64 — Most incredible event of trial was jailbreak at courthouse. Seven prisoners, including David Gregory, holding toy gun in hostage's back, bid for freedom. Gregory was captured, others made transitory escape.

3/8/64 — Defense witness stripper Pat Kohs was held on dope charge.

3/14/64 — With TV cameras grinding, Judge Brown read verdict.

3/14/64 — Jack Ruby shows no emotion as death verdict is passed.

3/19/64 — Following trial, Ruby family hired attorney Percy Foreman (left) to handle appeal. After only four days on case, Foreman retired, was replaced by Dr. Hubert Winston Smith (right), director of law science at U. of Texas.

3/1/64 — Thousands of Puerto Rican demonstrators march across Brooklyn Bridge to office of New York City Board of Education to urge improvement of educational facilities for Puerto Rican students.

3/2/64 — Ron and Steve Tollner (left and center), with friend, test radiophone at Stateline (Cal.) airport which is serving as rescue center for missing Paradise Airlines plane with 85 aboard, including the Tolliners' parents.

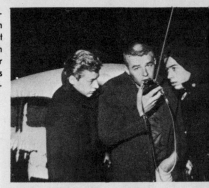

3/3/64 — Arizona Senator Barry Goldwater relaxes in Nashua, N. H., during his campaign for votes in that state's Republican presidential primary, the first in the country this year.

3/7/64 — New York Governor Nelson Rockefeller and wife "Happy" greet voters in New Hampshire, prior to primary. Despite intensive campaigns by Goldwater and Rockefeller, Henry Cabot Lodge won on write-in.

3/3/64 — Boys will be boys, even those who sport crutches and meet President Johnson in the White House. Performing for the President are Easter Seal twins, Ronnie and Donnie Cooper, a pair of spunky 6-year-olds from Colo. Looking on are comedian Bob Hope, the National Easter Seal Chairman, and J. P. W. Brown, head of the National Society for Crippled Children.

3/4/64 — International Teamster president James Hoffa (left) grits teeth after being found guilty of jury-tampering in Chattanooga, Tenn. Successful prosecuting team — first to convict Hoffa on a federal charge (in 5 tries) — are (L to R) James Neal, J. H. Reddy, Mr. and Mrs. John Hooker. Hoffa drew 8 years, $10,000 fine.

3/7/64 — While porter vacuums carpet, civil rights demonstrators conduct peaceful, and restful, sleep-in in lobby of a San Francisco hotel.

3/7/64 — Joseph Amsler, Barry Keenan and John Irwin leave Los Angeles court after conviction in Frank Sinatra Jr. kidnaping case. Amsler, Keenan got life. Irwin not convicted on kidnap count, found guilty on five others.

3/9/64 — Senate inquiry into "Frauds and the Elderly" draws testimony from Federal Drug Administration official, showing metal spike removed from hip of elderly patient because it rusted. It was one of a group of "quack" exhibits.

3/12/64—Cincinnati's River Downs Race Track was photo-finish-wire deep in waters of the Ohio River, which burst its banks in worst flood in 20 years. Some 30,000 families were made homeless along 560-mile stretch.

3/12/64 — Customers queue up for tickets as the nation's first legalized lottery in this century began in New Hampshire. Ticket dispensing machines were set up at Rockingham Park race track where "Sweepstakes" race will be held. Governor John King purchased first ticket.

3/16/64 — Gigantic brush fire roars out of control on the Verdugo Hills in Eagle Rock, Calif. Blaze claimed 30 homes, $5,000,000 damage in 40 hours.

3/25/64 — Salvo capabilities of Army Air Defense Command's Nike Hercules missile are revealed here. When one is fired, another is cocked, will blast off within seconds. They are to be used in defending against attack by bombers.

3/20/64 — Former Presidential Press Secretary Pierre Salinger confers with campaign aide after announcing his candidacy for Democratic nomination for U. S. Senator from California. Foes challenged legal aspects, courts upheld him.

3/25/64 — North Viet Nam stamp, depicting man and woman firing at U. S. helicopter, was branded "a blatant act of hostility toward U. S." by "Philately," a magazine for stamp collectors.

3/24/64 — Woman takes cover during stone-throwing racial demonstration outside Jacksonville's all-Negro New Stanton High School. This was climax to week of violence in which two were killed, 492 Negroes arrested. Formation of bi-racial committee to "resolve differences" ended the rioting.

3/25/64 — Annie Glenn, wife of Astronaut John Glenn, flashes election smile in Ohio after taking over campaign for Democratic Senate nomination for husband, who is recuperating in hospital from fall.

3/25/64 – College students twist-'n-sun on beach at Fort Lauderdale, Fla., during spring vacation. They are just part of annual migration of thousands to Florida resorts during Easter holidays.

3/28/64 – Debris and mud clutter street in Crescent City, Calif. after series of tidal waves hit coast city, leaving nine dead, 70 injured.

3/28/64 – Out for day of skiing at Stowe, Vermont, is Mrs. Jacqueline Kennedy. Occasion was Kennedy family gathering at resort over Easter.

ALASKA EARTHQUAKE

3/29/64 — "The earth started to roll," said one woman, and indeed it did. In places it cracked, in others it surged, all as part of one of the worst earthquakes on record. The site of the devastation was Alaska, but the effects were felt even thousands of miles away as tidal waves hit California (opposite page), Hawaii. Downtown Anchorage (above) suddenly became split-level; Seward was devastated by tidal waves, fire in addition to quake. Damage ran over $350 million, and all but crippled state's economy. Federal aid was given. Miraculously, loss of life was low.

NATIONAL NEWS-END

CYPRUS

3/26/64 — Despite calls for populace to surrender arms, both Greek and Turkish Cypriots still carry weapons on tension-torn island. Here Turkish-Cypriot shepherd totes shotgun while tending flock.

3/14/64 — Two Turkish-Cypriots dash across open field to join besieged comrades during fighting in Nicosia. Fierce clash at Ghaziveran drew threat from Turkey to intervene, drove small girl (right) from home.

3/1/64 – Austrian mountain rescue team (lower right) reaches wreckage of "Britannia" airliner, which slammed into Mt. Glungezer on Feb. 29, killing all 83 persons on board.

3/1/64 – Crewmen abandon Liberian tanker "Amphialos" which snapped in two in wild North Atlantic storm, 200 miles southwest of Halifax, Nova Scotia. Thirtyfour were rescued, 2 died.

3/2/64 – With steel shields for protection, Peruvian police assault battalion prepares to drive farm workers from cotton plantation in Piura. Top photo shows workers, with long knives flashing, retreating from field. They were protesting government land reforms.

3/4/64 – Framed by British barbed wire, Soviet troops parade before Russian War Memorial in British sector of West Berlin on 46th anniversary of Communist Army. English erected wire around monument in retaliation for Communists' wall.

3/9/64 — King Constantine, 23, and Queen Mother Frederika of Greece lead funeral procession for King Paul I, who died in Athens, at 62, of thrombosis of the lungs after 17-year reign. Former U. S. President Harry Truman attended funeral.

3/8/64 — Defense Secretary Robert McNamara (left) makes statement upon arrival for fact-finding tour in Viet Nam. In center is U.S. Ambassador Henry Cabot Lodge. Two days later, Lodge won New Hampshire primary.

3/9/64 — Rickshaws go up in flames in Zanzibar. New leftist government ordered them burned to abolish using men as beasts of burden.

3/16/64 — Huge crowd gathers in Mexico City to hear French President Charles De Gaulle speak to them in Spanish. He spent four days there, invited Mexico to go "hand in hand" with France.

3/23/64 — Peruvian military-surveying expedition, attempting to reach Yaravi River boat were surrounded by hostile Indians for eight days. United States Marine helicopter evacuates wounded from jungle camp site.

3/20/64 — Tug boats help launch 3,800-ton French nuclear submarine "Gymnote" at Cherbourg. She will test under water firing of polaris-type missles.

3/20/64 — Navy officers and police guard Russian-built helicopter in Key West after it was flown there by two Cuban Air Force defectors. They killed pilot, brought body here.

3/21/64 — After Brazilian Communists threatened general strike if nation's constitution was not changed, half million anti-leftists staged huge rally in downtown Sao Paulo in support of current constitution and democracy.

3/21/64 — U.S. Air Force 1st Lt. Harold Welch is carried on stretcher after release by Soviets in West Germany. His plane was shot down over East Germany. He broke arm, leg in parachute jump.

3/23/64 — Officials of International Commission view bodies of Cambodian villagers killed during Mar. 19 raid on border town by South Vietnamese troops. U. S. military observers were present during attack which was in error. U. S. issued an apology.

3/23/64 — Flag of city of Hamburg flies in breeze as West Germany's first post-war destroyer, the "Hamburg," is commissioned. The 2,850 ton ship can do 36 knots.

3/24/64 — U. S. Ambassador Edwin Reischauer is wheeled from Tokyo operating room after being stabbed (not seriously) by 19-year-old former mental patient (insert). Japanese Premier apologized to U. S. via Telstar.

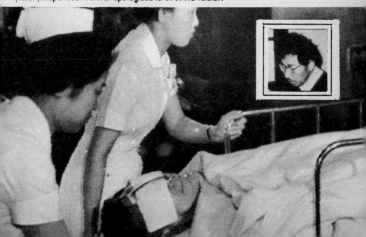

3/26/64 — Young men struggle to get into Army recruiting office in Kenya. Acute unemployment is stimulus to most to join up, even though mutiny last month was based, in part, on low pay.

3/31/64 — Nikita Khrushchev meets with Hungarian leaders in Budapest. Purpose of meeting was to develop strategy, reinforce ties for ideological dispute with the Red Chinese.

3/25/64 — In three years of America's Alliance for Progress aid program, close to $3 billion has been distributed to Central and South American nations. Amounts received by each country are indicated on map. Brazil has received the most, nearly half a billion; Haiti the least, some 16 million.

INTERNATIONAL NEWS—END

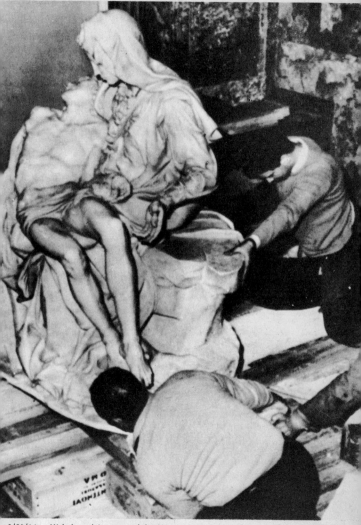

3/31/64 — Michelangelo's statue of the Pieta, a treasure beyond price, is moved off its pedestal in the Vatican, using soaped planks. The 6,700-pound masterpiece will be displayed at New York World's Fair.

3/1/64 — World featherweight champion Sugar Ramos knocks down Japanese challenger Mitsunori Seki for second time in sixth round to score technical knockout in title fight in Tokyo. Ramos, a Cuban now living in Mexico City, was making second defense of his crown.

3/10/64 — Actress Rosalind Russell clowns it up for members of Harvard's Hasty Pudding Club after they gave her "woman of year" award in Cambridge, Mass. Miss Russell's husband, Fred Brisson (light suit) looks on.

3/6/64 — Loyola University runner Tom O'Hara hits tape at Chicago Daily News Relays to lower world indoor mile record he set last month. Putting on strong finishing kick, Tom ran 3:56.4, two ticks under record.

3/17/64 — Richard Burton and Elizabeth Taylor show wedding rings to photographers at press conference in Toronto. They were secretly married two days before in Montreal. They will leave soon for Boston where Burton will play lead role in "Hamlet."

3/15/64 — Surrealist artist Salvadore Dali (right) and Mr. and Mrs. Huntington Hartford in latter's new New York gallery. Dali mural is backdrop.

3/22/64 — Comedienne Carol Burnett and film star Tina Louise rehearse for Broadway opening of "Fade Out, Fade In," spoof on movie musicals of '30s.

3/5/64 — Yankee slugger Mickey Mantle limbers up in spring training. His knee operation last fall was sixth time he's had surgery in 12 seasons.

3/16/64 — 1963 Rookies of the Year, Chicago White Sox pitcher Gary Peters (left) and Cincinnati infielder Pete Rose receive their awards in Tampa.

3/3/64 — Opera singer Patrice Munsel models "open back" gold pajamas by Courreges at benefit fashion show in Studio City, Calif.

3/22/64 — UCLA's Walt Hazzard unhooks net after Bruins completed unbeaten year, winning NCAA tourney in Kansas City.

3/26/64 — World-famous Venus de Milo is snapped from all angles by photographers after arrival from France at Tokyo's Ueno Western Museum. Statue was "slightly damaged" during her journey.

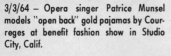

3/31/64 — Detroit Red Wing star Gordie Howe takes spill in front of Chicago goal during Stanley Cup semifinal series. Fourth-place Wings won series, then lost seven-game final to Toronto Maple Leafs.

3/23/64—Honor student, Yvonne Burgess, 16, jumps (inset) from 4th story of John Jay high school, Brooklyn, N.Y. Caught in police net, she was rushed to hospital.

3/27/64 — Hidden camera in Toronto bank recorded gun play in holdup. Top left, detective Robert Dixon grabs bandit (hat on). Top right, bandit fires on Dixon, grazing him. Lower right, Dixon arises, shoots bandit in back of head, killing him.

MISCELLANY

3/15/64 — Mountain climbers in Argentina display petrified body, presumably of young boy who died some 400 years ago, near the summit of "El Torro."

3/10/64 — Nurse checks condition of Mrs. Marie Adams, 45, who was brought to Tulsa hospital day before, apparently frozen to death. Doctors found no heartbeat and body temperature was below 67 degrees.

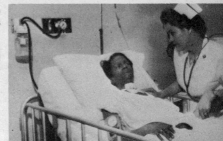

3/10/64 — When 1,500-pound Hereford steer broke loose in Chicago slaughterhouse, employee Mucio Zacharias, a native of Mexico who fought bulls as a boy, wore out the animal with deft capework, finally forcing him to his knees. He then tied the beast up.

3/27/64 — Lives of seemingly doomed cancer victims are being prolonged by use of a pump (shown here) which patients carry in breast pocket, like hearing aid. It pumps diluted anti-cancer drug into artery which supplies liver with blood. Dr. Robert Sullivan of Boston's Lahey Clinic developed pump.

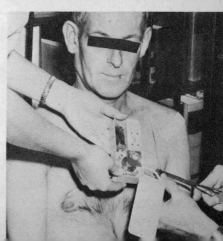

3/9/64 — Ace parachutist Donald West (top) falls to death in Adelaide, Australia, trying to set world baton-passing record. He just passed baton to man below him, delayed opening chute to try for another pass. A third parachutist took the picture.

3/18/64 — "Oh My Golly" (on rail) starts to go down in first race at Aqueduct Race Track after its ankle snapped, as can be seen in photo. Jockey Don Pierce braces for fall. Animal had to be destroyed.

MARCH – END

SUMMARY-APRIL 1964

NATIONAL

General of the Army Douglas MacArthur, 60 years an army officer, died at the age of 84 (April 3). Pressinterviews given by the five star general some years earlier and released posthumously, contained accusations that the British betrayed the U.S. in the Korean War and that the U.S. State Department had "robbed the allies of victory." Both charges were denied by the British and by Secretary of State Dean Rusk and Maj. General Courtney Whitney, former aide to General MacArthur.

The United States and Panama agreed (April 3) to resume diplomatic relations which had been suspended by Panama following anti-U.S. riots over an incident involving the raising of the U.S. flag in the U.S. zone without an accompanying Panamanian flag..... An agreement to study a new sea-level canal linking the Atlantic and Pacific oceans was signed (April 16) by Colombia and the U.S.

The U.S. Supreme Court ruled that former Mississippi governor Ross R. Barnett and his successor Paul B. Johnson would have to stand trial in federal court on contempt charges without a jury. The charges stemmed from resistance to the entrance of Negro James Meredith into the University of Mississippi in 1963 ..... The second trial of Byron de la Beckwith for the killing of Medgar Evers, official of the National Association for the Advancement of Colored People (NAACP), in Jackson, Miss. ended (April 17) like the first in a mistrial when an all-white jury was unable to reach a verdict..... A so-called "white backlash" against Negro civil rights demonstrations was the explanation given by expert observers for Gov. George C. Wallace of Alabama receiving 23 per cent of votes cast in the Wisconsin Democratic presidential primary.... the Brooklyn N.Y. branch of the Congress for Racial Equality (CORE) called on its members (April 9) to block the five major routes to the New York World's Fair on opening day (April 22) by having their cars run out of gas. James R. Farmer, national president of CORE, immediately suspended the branch which responded by urging a tie-up of the main rail routes to the Fair..... The threats failed to materialize and the Fair opened on schedule (April 22) in a heavy downpour ..... The Pentagon ended enrollment of military personnel, except for members of the Reserve Officers Training Corps (ROTC) in all schools, colleges and Universities which practiced racial discrimination..... Catholic Archbishop Thomas J. Toolen of the Birmingham-Mobile, Alabama, diocese ordered desegregation of all schools under his jurisdiction with the beginning of the school year in September.

Eight of the largest steel companies and two of their officials were indicted by the federal government on charges of fixing the prices of carbon steel sheet which is used mainly in consumer products and accounts for annual sales of $2 billion..... **The nation's waiters** protested to the Internal Revenue Bureau that the average tip which the Bureau had been estimating for tax purposes at 15% of the check was actually closer to 7.5%.

The five-year-old work rules dispute on the railroads erupted (April 8) into a walkout by employees of the Illinois Central Railroad which threatened to escalate into a nation-wide stoppage of railroad traffic. The next day **President Lyndon B. Johnson** obtained a 15-day postponement of the walk-out and a week later arranged a permanent settlement of the dispute..... **The Teamsters Union** stopped paying (April 27) the legal expenses of its chief, **James R. Hoffa**, appealing a conviction for jury tampering and facing trial for conspiracy and fraud in connection with teamster pension funds..... **President Johnson** announced (April 16) that gross national product for the first quarter was running at the record rate of $608 billion a year and General Motors reported first quarter profits of $536 million ..... On April 30, the **economic boom** had lasted 38 months, longer than any boom since the end of World War II.

Governor William W. Scranton of Pennsylvania announced (April 9) that he would accept the nomination for president on the Republican ticket if he were drafted..... **Senator Barry Goldwater** of Arizona suffered a setback by winning only 66% of the votes in the Illinois primaries, according to the experts, since unknown **Senator Margaret Chase Smith** of Maine received 25% of the vote from anti-Goldwater Republicans.

The U.S. Defense Department reported an overwhelming superiority over the Soviet Union in missiles and bombers with 750 long range missiles against 188 for the Soviets, 540 bombers against 240 and 192 Polaris missiles with a range of 1500 miles against an unknown but smaller number of submarine mounted missiles with a range of 500 miles.

Hollywood awarded its Oscars to: Patricia Neal, best actress, in **Hud**; Sidney Poitier, first Negro to win top Oscar, best actor, in **Lillies of the Field**; Tony Richardson, best director, for **Tom Jones**; and to **Tom Jones**, best picture.

The trial of Roy Cohn, former chief aide to Senator Joseph McCarthy, in Federal court for perjury ended in a mistrial when a juror was excused because of the death of her father..... **Former Republican Governor of Illinois, William G. Stratton**, was indicted (April 15) on a charge of evading federal income taxes amounting to $46,676, for the years 1957-60..... **Twentieth-Century-Fox**, producers of the movie, Cleopatra, sued Elizabeth Taylor for $20 million dollars for breach of contract during the filming of the picture, and sued Liz and Richard Burton as a team for another $30 million for depreciating the value of the movie by scandalous conduct during and before the filming..... **Lowell M. Birrell**, charged with stock swindles and tax evasion in the millions of dollars, left his haven in Brazil and returned to the U.S. to face trial.

The cigarette industry agreed to a code forbidding appeals to people under 21 and implications that cigarette smoking aids health or virility..... **President Johnson** shocked dog-lovers of the world when he lifted his pet beagles by the ears to make them yelp..... **Peter Lawford**, married to a sister of the late President Kennedy, was turned down as a tenant of a swank New York co-operative apartment for being an actor and a Democrat.

INTERNATIONAL

In Belgium, 10,000 doctors and 2,000 dentists went on strike (April 1) against new health legislation which drastically cut medical fees. When a 15-month-old baby died, two doctors were arrested on charges of criminal negligence and on April 12, the Belgian Government mobilized doctors in the army reserves and ordered 3,000 of them back to work. A few days later the strike was called off.

Joao Goulart, President of Brazil, was ousted by the army (April 1). His temporary successor was the President of the Chamber of Deputies and he, in turn, gave way to 63-year-old General **Humberto Castelo Branco**, one of the leaders of the successful coup. The new government arrested 7,000 in a drive against "reds" and deprived three generals, two former presidents, 46 congressmen and 60 other officials of the right to vote or hold office.

The Communist Party of the Soviet Union expelled Vyacheslav Molotov, former foreign secretary, Georgi M. Malenkov, former Premier, and former Deputy-Premier Lazar M. Kaganovich, for anti-party activities..... **A rumor that Premier Nikita Khrushchev** had died swept world (April 13)..... Four days later K. celebrated his 70th birthday.

The neutralist government of Prime Minister Souvanna Phouma **in Laos was overthrown** (April 19) by rightist militarists. Under pressure from the U.S. the militarists restored the Prime Minister to office when he agreed to include rightists representatives in his coalition government. On April 28, dissenting leftists launched a military attack against rightists forces.

Princess Irene of the Netherlands defied her parents and her government to marry (April 29) in Rome, Prince Carlos of Bourbon Palma, claimant to the throne of Spain.

National elections for Britain were set for October when the five-year mandate of the current Conservative Government led by Sir Alec Douglas-Home, Prime Minister, expires. As the announcement was made (April 9), bookmakers were offering odds of five to one on a Labor Party victory.

Tanganyika in East Africa and the island republic of Zanzibar merged (April 26) into the United Republic of Taganyika and Zanzibar. Tanganyikan President Julius Nyerere became President of the new country.

SPORTS

Dallas Long broke his own world's record of 65 feet 10 inches for the shot put in Los Angeles with a toss of 65 feet 11 1/2 inches (April 4).

Castro Ortiz outpointed Kenny Lane in a 15-round bout in San Juan, Puerto Rico, to retain the World's Lightweight Boxing crown. (April 11)

Arnold Palmer won (April 12) his fourth Masters Title in Augusta, Ga., with a score of 276, six strokes ahead of Jack Nicklaus and Dave Marr.

Ken Johnson of the Houston Colts pitched (April 23) a no-hitter against the Cincinnati Reds but lost the game 1-0 in the ninth inning on two errors by the Colts.

Al Oerter broke his own discus throwing record of 205 feet 5-1/2 inches with a throw of 206 feet 6 inches during the Mount San Antonio Relays in Walnut, Cal.

OBITUARIES

John Haynes Holmes, 84, a Unitarian minister for 60 years who helped bring about the Seabury investigation of Mayor James J. Walker of New York, and who was a founder of the National Association for the Advancement of Colored People (NAACP) and the American Civil Liberties Union. (April 3)

Rachel Carson, 56, author of "Silent Spring" which sparked a government investigation of pesticides. (April 14)

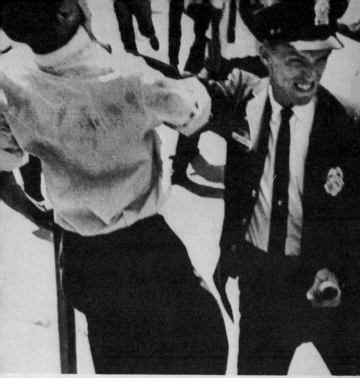

4/28/64 — A Nashville, Tenn. policeman stiff-arms Negro demonstrator after he refused to move from path of police paddy wagon, loaded with other demonstrators. Police had to use force to disperse crowd of 300. (See page 101 for other photos.)

NATIONAL NEWS

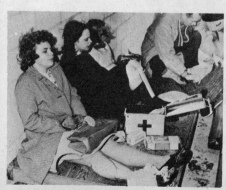

4/2/64 — Young girls await first aid after being injured on escalator in Baltimore stadium. Guard bar at top of stairs had not been removed when school children swarmed aboard. One died, 22 were hurt.

4/2/64 — Two young girls peer into 50-foot crevice in downtown Anchorage. It has widened since quake.

4/8/64 — President Johnson pays homage to General Douglas MacArthur by placing wreath at hero's casket in Capitol rotunda. General died 4/5 at age 84 from acute kidney, liver failure.

4/1/64 — Interior of Boeing space chamber after five men emerged from 30-day simulated flight in Seattle. Equipment shown is waste disposal and water reclaiming system, which collected water from body waste, condensation; purified it for reuse.

4/13/64 — Space veteran Virgil (Gus) Grissom (front left) and former test pilot John W. Young will man two-seater Gemini spaceship on three-day orbit, possibly before Xmas. Walter Schirra, Thomas Stafford are backup crew.

4/7/64 — Pan American jetliner pilot Herbert Dunker and two crew members trudge through marshes after his craft skidded off runway upon landing at JFK Airport. Plane cracked in two; 46 of 150 were hurt.

4/1/64 — Mrs. Malcolm Peabody, mother of Massachusetts governor is released from jail in St. Augustine, Fla., after she participated in bi-racial demonstration at restaurant. St. John County sheriff bids her farewell.

4/7/64 — Rev. Bruce William Klunder, 26, was crushed to death by bulldozer in Cleveland while demonstrating against school segregation. He and three others tried to immobilize bulldozer on construction project. Three lay in front of the machine, the Rev. Klunder in back.

4/7/64 — Rev. Klunder's body lies in mud after bulldozer backed over him (driver did not know he was there). Klunder's group was protesting new school in Negro neighborhood, which, they said prompted segregation. After death of Presbyterian minister, mobs rioted; city officials promised school study.

4/10/64 — Mrs. Verda Welcome, Maryland's only Negro state senator, was shot and wounded as she left church meeting in Baltimore.

4/15/64 — Mrs. Jerrie Mock, 38-year-old mother and housewife, arrives home in Columbus, O., after becoming first woman to fly solo around the world.

4/9/64 — In eerie half-light of construction lamps, crews labor in center cavern of North American Air Defense Command's underground headquarters in Colorado

4/22/64 — Civil rights demonstrations marred opening of World's Fair in Flushing Meadow, but threatened stall-in of automobiles on highways to and from Fair did not come off. Coupled with bad weather, threat of stall-in did keep crowds small (less than 100,000). Militant integrationists circled Fair's symbol, the Unisphere, demonstrated at Fair gates (left), and chanted "Freedom Now" as President Johnson dedicated Federal Pavilion. In all, 294 demonstrators were arrested. Despite this, most visitors agreed Fair, which was some 44 months under construction and cost $500 million, was a success. Though some exhibits were not completed at opening, major pavilions were open.

4/23/64 — "USS Henry Clay," an American nuclear - powered submarine, demonstrates capability of firing Polaris missile from surface off Cape Kennedy, Fla. In space of 30 minutes, submarine fired missile while submerged, then launched one from the surface. Objects in air around missile are launch adapters designed to detach once missile is fired.

4/23/64 — Fugitive financier Lowell M. Birrell is taken into custody by FBI agents upon arrival in New York from Brazil to face fraud and income tax evasion charges. Birrell fled to Cuba in 1957, spent last five years in Brazil after being charged with defrauding Dynamics Corp. of America of some $3.2 million and evading $3.7 million in federal income taxes.

4/25/64 — Injured state trooper is led to safety by fellow troopers on fifth night of violent civil rights demonstrations against school segregation in Chester, Pa. At right Negro crawls from night-stick swinging police. Scores were arrested.

4/24/64 — President and Mrs. Johnson greet family of unemployed saw mill worker in Inez, Kentucky, during five-state tour of poverty-stricken area. President told father of eight to keep his children in school.

4/28/64 — Civil rights demonstrator is chased by club-wielding police in downtown Nashville, Tenn., on second day of demonstrations outside local restaurant.

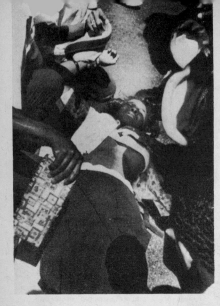

4/28/64 – Civil rights demonstrators aid unconscious girl after she was injured in Nashville. Police used clubs to disperse anti-segregationists, then had to turn them on crowd of 1,000 whites which threatened to attack Negroes.

4/29/64 – Princess Irene of The Netherlands on her way to Vatican for private audience with Pope Paul VI after her marriage to Prince Carlos Hugo of Spain in Rome. Members of Dutch Royal family did not attend wedding for which Princess Irene converted to Catholicism, gave up rights to throne.

4/29/64 – Mrs. Andres Mejias (being lowered in a litter), one of nine Cuban refugees fleeing island in small boat and rescued by British frigate, HMS "Tatar", is transferred to U.S. Coast Guard boat after giving birth to a daughter off Miami.

4/30/64 — Mural depicting Arab boy and his mother pleading for aid, created controversy at World's Fair. It is on display at Jordanian Pavilion. New York Mayor Robert Wagner said mural would have to be eliminated after Jews complained it was anti-Israel. Jordan officials refused. Fair was caught in middle, but took no action.

4/27/64 — Dr. J. L. West (at right) and Jack Ruby's defense attorney Dr. Hubert Smith talk to reporters after hearing on motion to have Ruby committed to hospital for mental tests. Dr. West said Ruby believed Jews were being slain in America because of him. Court ordered psychiatric exam.

NATIONAL NEWS-END

INTERNATIONAL NEWS

4/3/64 — The young man with all the hair is neither Ringo Starr nor any other Beatle. It's Prince Charles arriving at London Airport from Glasgow for weekend visit with his parents, Queen Elizabeth and Prince Philip.

BRAZILIAN REVOLT

4/1/64 – Rebel elements of Brazilian Army stand guard in Belo Horizonte where revolt against leftist government of President Joao Goulart began. City lies north of Rio de Janerio. Rebels hoped to draw Goulart's forces there, then march on Rio.

4/1/64 – Tactics work as First Army leaves Rio to engage rebels in Belo Horizonte and other trouble spots in state of Minas Gerais. When First Army reached insurgent forces they joined rebellion.

4/2/64 – Soon 14 states were in open rebellion. Goulart fled to nation's capital, remote city of Brasilia. After situation became worse he escaped seeking asylum in Uruguay. 300,000 danced in streets.

4/2/64 – Four hours after Goulart left Brasilia, joint session of Congress named Ranieri Mazzilli Provisional President, next in line according to constitution which Goulart wanted to re-write.

4/15/64 – Two weeks later, Mazzilli turns sash of office over to new president, Gen. Castelo Branco, who will serve out Goulart's term. Next elections are due in 1965.

4/23/64 – Communist-led Brazilian Marines (in tee-shirts) are "read out" of Corps as general purge of leftists. They had revolted in March, but were praised, not punished by Goulart.

4/21/64 — Newsmap of Brazil shows vast natural resources of nation, which is the largest in South America (as big as America's first 48 states, with population of some 78 million). Nation is already world's leading producer of coffee, also has vast reserves of timber, petroleum, iron ore and other metals. Grasslands of the southern states support huge herds of cattle. Country's biggest difficulties are runaway inflation (cost of living soared 300 percent in 31 months under Goulart), widespread poverty, illiteracy and lagging social and economic reforms. U. S. promised aid to new government.

SOUTH AMERICA

BRAZIL

AMAZON RIVER

BRAZIL

SUGAR

MINING

PETROLEUM

CATTLE

COFFEE

TIMBER

INDUSTRY

BRASILIA

RIO DE JANE

SAO PAULO

ATLANTIC OC

PORTO ALEGRE

4/3/64 — Wilhelm Bogner (glasses) sits in well-guarded West German court where he is being tried for his part in Nazi atrocities. Bogner, now 56, was known as "torture master" at Auschwitz concentration camp. Witness said he was "a born sadist, who didn't mind killing people. It was all in a day's work for him." Once he killed mutinous Jewish inmates, one by one.

4/3/64 — With members of the National Security Council looking on, President Johnson speaks by telephone with Panamanian President Roberto Chiari. Afterwards, President Johnson announced U. S. and Panama have decided to re-establish diplomatic relations, and discuss ways to settle Canal dispute.

4/3/64 — Finland's Sakari Tuomioja (left) shakes hands with Cyprus President Archbishop Makarios. Tuomioja has been assigned as U. N. mediator to settle Cyprus dispute between Greeks and Turks.

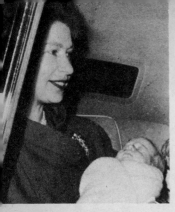

4/4/64 — Queen Elizabeth leaves Buckingham Palace by car with newest member of the Royal family, month-old prince, who at time of picture, was still unnamed. He is fourth child, third son of the British Queen.

4/7/64 — Six plunged to watery death when supertanker "Esso Maracaibo" rammed into Mile-long Urdaneta bridge in Venezuela. Collision, which occurred at midnight, toppled one of the concrete piers supporting bridge, which is longest in world, 1,500-foot section collapsed.

4/5/64 — Soviet Premier Nikita Khrushchev shakes hands with unidentified priest at reception of the Presidium of the Hungarian People's Republic in Budapest. Event marked the 19th anniversary of Hungary's liberation from the Nazis. At right is Premier Kadar.

4/4/64 — Huge billboard-like frame, built on border of East and West Berlin, will soon flash latest news to people living in Eastern sector of city. Built on hilltop, it will give news in illuminated moving letters, visible from a considerable distance.

4/14/64 — King Hussein of Jordan greets President and Mrs. Johnson at White House where state dinner was given in his honor. Following dinner, jazz concert was given for the King, who is music fan. Guests then danced.

4/15/64 — Bikini-clad girl finds armed guard on board pleasure craft off Havana. Guards are placed on all boats by government to prevent defections.

4/15/64 — Two faces of Havana. Above, militia woman stands guard at public building. Such service is voluntary, calling for either four hours duty at day, or two hours at night. At right, Havana nightlife, once a big tourist attraction, continues, but night club revues like the one at the Rivera Club are somewhat subdued.

4/11/64 — Soviet "Guideline" missile, a surface-to-air rocket, blasts off on firing range. It travels twice the speed of sound, is similar to U. S. Ajax-Nike.

4/14/64 — Greek Cypriot police take up positions on Ledra Street (Murder Mile) in Nicosia after fighting broke out anew between Greek and Turkish Cypriots. Outbreak was marked by scuffle between Greeks and British troops, serving in name of U. N.

4/18/64 — Laos' neutralist Prime Minister Souvanna Phouma (center) on day before right-wing generals, including Gen. Phoumi Nosavan (at right), seized him, announced his resignation. Five days later, the generals bowed to international pressure, agreed to let Phouma continue as head of government. At left is Pathet Lao's Prince Souphanouvong.

4/21/64 — Rare tribute to U. S. was paid by Czechoslovakia which issued four stamps of different denominations, honoring American astronauts Wally Schirra (left), Scott Carpenter (top), John Glenn (bottom) and Gordon Cooper (right)

4/19/64 — Specially-trained team goes about dangerous business of excavating some 32,000 mustard-gas shells hidden by Germans during World War II near Vienna. City's water supply was endangered by shells. Excavation work could only be done during extremely good weather, with proper wind conditions.

INTERNATIONAL NEWS-END

ENTERTAINMENT, SPORTS & THE ARTS

4/1/64 — Brigitte Bardot and boy-friend Bob Zaguri stroll hand-in-hand in Brazilian fishing village of Buzios. Miss Bardot requested photos be taken here to answer charge in recent Brazilian magazine that she was "fat, ugly and sunburned." Reports seem in error.

4/12/64 — Even brides cry at weddings as rock n' roll star Chubby Checker discovers when his wife, 22-year-old, former Miss World, Catherine Lodders, bursts into tears at church in Pennsauken, N.J.

4/2/64 – A. J. Foyt (right) of Houston receives "Outstanding Achievement Award" as nation's top automobile racer during 1963 at dinner in New York. Presenting award is Tony Hulman, head of Indianapolis Speedway.

4/16/64 – British actor Peter Sellers and wife, Swedish actress Britt Ekland in Sellers' Hollywood hospital room. He is recuperating from a severe coronary thrombosis attack in which his heart stopped beating eight times.

4/10/64 – Light-heavyweight champion Willie Pastrano (left) lands right to face of challenger Gregorio Peralta of Argentina in title fight at New Orleans. Pastrano retained title on 6th round technical knockout, when Peralta suffered eye cut.

4/12/64 – Arnold Palmer sports victory smile as Jack Nicklaus helps him into green blazer, symbol of his victory in Master's Golf Tournament at Augusta, Ga. Triumph was Palmer's fourth in Master's, and his most impressive, as he beat Nicklaus, the defending champion, and Dave Marr by six strokes.

4/23/64 – More than 2,700 celebrities, including state and city officials, attend opening of New York State Theatre, the second completed component in New York City's Lincoln Center for the Performing Arts. First night program in $19.3 million theatre was performance by New York City ballet, plus scene from "Carousel."

4/18/64 — American actress Carroll Baker tries on fur coat in Paris salon. She went there, prior to premiere of "The Carpetbaggers," to get $100,000 dress.

2/13/64 — President Johnson munches popcorn, talks to House Speaker John McCormack on opening day of baseball season. Senators lost to Angels, 4-0.

4/14/64 — Patricia Neal, winner of Academy Award for best actress of the year, arrives in London from her home near there. Married to British writer Roald Dahl, Miss Neal is expecting a child in six weeks. Below, actor Sidney Poitier, winner of best actor Oscar, visits director Ralph Nelson (left), who directed his winning role. Nelson was in process of directing Cary Grant and Leslie Caron in new film.

4/30/64 — Four of seven men who shared in largest pari-mutuel payoff in history toast one of four horses — Historic Value — who helped them win $132,232.80 twin-double at Roosevelt Raceway 4/28.

4/26/64 — Tommy Heinsohn (left), coach Red Auerbach and Bill Russell are carried around Boston Garden court after Boston Celtics won sixth straight National Basketball Association championship, beating San Francisco Warriors in five games. Celtics are only pro team in history to win six in row.

4/26/64 — Judy Kimball (left) isn't mad at anyone but herself for missing putt in Titleholders' golf, but Marilyn Smith ducks anyway. Latter won tourney.

4/20/64 — Aurele Vandendriessche of Belgium gives victory salute as he approaches finish line of 68th annual Boston Marathon. His winning time for 26-mile, 385-yard race was a fast 2:19.59.

4/23/64 — Trainer works on ankle of Houston Colt pitcher Ken Johnson after he became first major leaguer to pitch no-hit game, and lose. Cincinnati beat him, 1-0, on two errors in ninth, one by Johnson.

4/16/64 – Charlie Chaplin who rose to fame as a pathetic tramp-clown (right) in early movie days, turned 75 on this day. Though best-known as a comedian, Chaplin was also a writer and composer, plus being a family man of some renown. The last of his seven children by Oona O'Neill (background) was born two years ago. A millionaire, he lives in Switzerland. Daughter Geraldine is with him above.

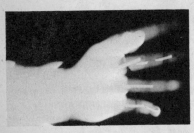

4/23/64 – Radiograph pictures taken by Eastman-Kodak team in Rome show that fingers on left-hand of Virgin Mary in Michelangelo's Famed Pieta were broken some time in past. Interior pins were used to reassemble fingers. Pictures were taken by process using gamma rays.

4/17/64 – U. S. Attorney General Robert F. Kennedy visits backstage with Carol Channing after her performance in musical comedy smash "Hello Dolly" in New York

4/28/64 — Walter McGowan of Scotland couldn't lift European flyweight boxing crown from head of Italy's Salvatore Burrini, so he did next best thing. He lifted Burrini in his arms after Rome fight. Crowd of 15,000 cheered sportsmanlike gesture.

4/27/64 — Replica of Denmark's famed "Little Mermaid" graces Danish Garden at New York's World's Fair, gift of Carlsberg Foundation, a scientific-cultural organization which had original sculpted. Over weekend, the original was decapitated in Copenhagen by vandals. Foundation will have a new head recast.

ENTERTAINMENT, SPORTS & THE ARTS-END

MISCELLANY

4/10/64 — Body of Arthur S. Daniels lies beneath car — allegedly stolen — which slipped off jack in Hallendale, Fla. He and Willie Johnson, also trapped under car, were allegedly stripping parts from car prior to accident in which both were killed. At left are a battery, radio and wheel removed from car.

4/20/64 — Three school girls look at mummified body of girl who died some 1800 years ago in Rome. Body, which was discovered last month, is of 10-year-old. It is now on display in Rome Museum.

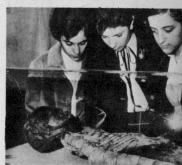

4/14/64 — Australian Michael Rubbo comforts Mary Ann Kelley, 23, after their cars collided head-on in Woodside, Calif. A Stanford student, Rubbo admitted driving on left side of road, as they do in Australia, from force of habit. He escaped from his car, pulled Miss Kelley from hers before both caught fire. She died.

4/22/64 — Abdel Razzik Hifny, 21, of Cairo, Egypt, after learning he may expect to inherit $1 million for generous gesture he made to tourist when he was a Cairo newsboy. Seems his benefactor, the late Richard Keev of Los Angeles, arrived in Cairo, wanted to buy paper, but had no local currency. He offered boy American dollar, but Abdel said he couldn't accept it, made gift of paper to Keev. Latter didn't forget gesture, returned to Cairo to send boy to school.

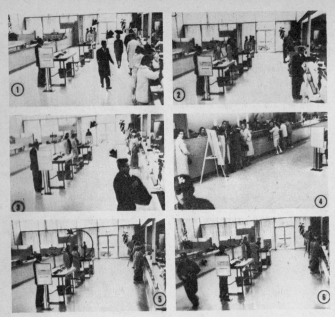

4/3/64 — Holdup in bank at Encino, Calif., is caught by camera. Photo 1 shows one of three bandits approaching teller's cage with revolver in hand, while confederate (rear) holds shotgun in back of two women. (2) Gunman directs tellers to fill bags and (3) grabs money. (4) Shotgun wielding bandit whirls to face camera, noise of which startled him. (5) He fires at camera, hits wall below, and (6) runs to rear of bank. Pictures led to capture and conviction of robbers.

4/3/64 — Discovery in East Africa of an entire new species of primitive human, believed to be direct ancestor of modern man, was announced by British anthropologist Dr. Louis Leakey at National Geographic Society in Washington. Smaller than pygmies, but quite similar to modern man, species is believed to have existed 1 million years, beginning 2 million years ago. Skull at left is believed to be that of a young woman of the newly-discovered species, called homo habilis or "able man." Larger skull at right is that of a present day African. Remains of new species indicate well-formed feet, meaning creature walked erect. Dr. Leakey thinks homo habilis used tools and weapons.

4/10/64 — Ona Lee Fuller, 16, leaps from atop six-story building in New York into police nets; was taken unconscious to hospital.

APRIL – END

SUMMARY-MAY 1964

NATIONAL

A 14-year-old girl and 45 other children were hurt (May 2) at Baltimore Memorial Stadium following a baseball game between the Baltimore Orioles and Cleveland Indians when hundreds of youngsters panicked on finding that a moving stairway exit to which they had been directed was blocked at the top.

Governor George Wallace of Alabama received 28% of the votes in Indiana's Democratic Presidential primary (April 5). On the Republican side, Harold Stassen surprised observers by tallying 25% of the votes in a race against Senator Barry Goldwater..... Robert F. Taft Jr., son of "Mr. Republican", the late Senator Robert F. Taft, won a landslide victory in the race for the senatorial nomination on the Republican ticket in Ohio..... Mayor Robert F. Wagner announced (April 6) that he was available as a Democratic Vice-Presidential candidate if "President Lyndon B. Johnson wants me"..... Governor William W. Scranton of Pennsylvania indicated (April 6) that he would be willing to accept the second spot on a Republican ticket headed by Senator Goldwater..... Attorney General Robert F. Kennedy was reported considering (April 14) an invitation to run for a seat in the U.S. Senate in New York State..... Governor Nelson Rockefeller of New York was the winner over Senator Goldwater and Henry Cabot Lodge in Oregon's Republican primary..... Supporters of Henry Cabot Lodge for the Republican Presidential nomination announced that they would back Governor Rockefeller in the California primary..... Governor Wallace took 43% of the votes in Maryland's Democratic primary..... Former President Dwight D. Eisenhower released a description of the type of man he would like to see win the Republican Presidential nomination. Experts agreed that the description fitted all leading candidates except Senator Goldwater.

President Johnson waived retirement regulations to permit FBI Chief, J. Edgar Hoover, to keep his job after reaching the age of 70..... Their first child, a son, was born (May 30) on the eve of the California presidential primary to Governor Rockefeller of New York and his second wife "Happy".....

Goldwater statement that one of ways suggested to assist Viet Nam in war was use of atomic weapons to defoliate jungle thereby exposing Viet Cong lines of supply, was denounced in U.N. by Soviet delegate and U Thant (June 26).

Fred E. Black Jr., named as a Robert G. Baker associate in the investigation of the former Secretary to the Senate Democratic Majority by a Senate Rules Committee, was found guilty (May 5) of evading $91,000 in income taxes ..... Speaker John F. Thompson of the Massachussetts House of Representatives, a Democrat, was indicted along with 25 others on a charge of corrupt practices.....

Democratic Congressman Adam Clayton Powell of Harlem, N.Y. was ordered arrested by a New York judge for contempt of court in ignoring a libel judgment. The arrest order specified that it was not to take effect until Congress adjourned.....
The Special Counsel to the Senate Rules Committee investigating the affairs of Robert G. Baker reported (May 18) findings of gross impropriety and fraudulent practice but no conflict of interest warranting legal action..... **The Treasurer of the Shubert theater properties** in New York, consisting of 17 theaters, was arrested on a charge of having taken $70,000 from theater ticket brokers in 1963 for providing them with tickets to hit shows.

     Union plumbers walked out on a construction job in New York City when three Puerto Ricans and one Negro, all non-union workers, were added to the plumbing force. The dispute was settled when Mayor Wagner persuaded the union to let the four workers take the union's qualifying test. One of the workers refused to take the test, the other three flunked it..... **Fred O'Neal**, Negro actor, became (May 5) the first member of his race to head Actors Equity, trade union of the profession..... **The University of Texas** hired the **first Negro** member of its faculty..... **Dr. Elder G. Hawkins**, a Negro minister, scored another first for his race when he was elected head of the United Presbyterian Church which has 3.2 million members in the U.S., mostly whites..... The **public library** in New London, Conn. **purged its "Mother Goose" volumes** of all rhymes containing the word "nigger"..... Passengers on New York's subway and Staten Island Ferry were the victims of a wave of terrorism at the hands of young Negro hoodlums during the night of April 31.

     The New York State Supreme Court declared Mexican divorces invalid in the State when obtained by mutual agreement..... The U.S. Supreme Court nullified a law which deprived naturalized citizens of citizenship if they spent three years in the country of their birth or five years in any foreign country without returning to the U.S. An estimated 40,000 people were affected..... **Countrywide ceremonies marked the 10th anniversary** (May 18) of the Supreme Court's ruling against segregation in public schools.

     A 2,000-miles-per-hour bomber, the B-70, was given its first public showing in California (April 11)..... For the first time in 48 years, **no Pulitzer Prizes** were awarded for the novel, drama and music.

INTERNATIONAL

     Khrushchev warned the U.S. in a May Day speech that surveillance flights over Cuba could lead to war..... At the start (May 9) of a 16-day tour of the United Arab Republic, Khrushchev was hailed by President Nasser as "a courageous warrior". K. responded by denouncing **Israel as "a stooge of the imperialists"**..... Hundreds of **Czech students battled** with police in Prague in a demonstration **against the secret police** and for freedom..... **Red China** rejected (May 8) the Soviet Union's call for an early world conference of communist parties to resolve the differences between the two countries.

     Secretary of Defense Robert S. McNamara, on his return (May 12) from his fifth trip to South Viet Nam said the U.S. "will provide whatever is required for however long it takes to win the war in Viet Nam."..... **Secretary of State Dean Rusk** hinted in a speech (May 22) that the war in S. Viet Nam might be expanded to North Viet Nam..... Rightist and neutralist factions joined the Laos coalition government which was under attack by Red forces..... **The U.S. considered intervention** as Red forces threatened to over-run Laos..... Prince Souphanouvong, leader of the pro-Red Pathet Lao in Laos, quit the coalition government..... **France called for an East-West conference** to restore peace in Laos.

     In Panama, Marco A. Robles, the candidate favored by the government for the Presidency, defeated Dr. Arnulfo Arias..... **Brazil** severed (May 13) its ties with Castro's Cuba..... Victor Paz Estenssoro won (May 31) an uncontested second four-year term as President of Bolivia..... More than **300 were killed in Lima**, Peru (May 24) in a riot during a soccer game between Peru and Argentina.

     A Vatican newspaper and a Cardinal suggested that the Roman Catholic Church might re-examine the Church's position on birth control in view of the development of oral contraceptives.

     40 microphones were discovered hidden in the walls of the U.S. Embassy in Moscow. They had been there for 11 years.

SPORTS

     Northern Dancer, the second choice in the betting, won the Kentucky Derby (May 2). The first Canadian horse to win the Derby, Northern Dancer edged out the favorite, Hill Rise..... Two weeks later (May 16), Northern Dancer did it again in the Preakness, this time beating Hill Rise by a wider margin to take the second event in the so-called triple-crown of racing.

      The judges awarded **Sugar Ramos** of Cuba the victory by a split decision in a featherweight championship bout with Floyd Robertson of Ghana held in Ghana. Next day, **The Ghana Boxing Authority reversed the decision.**

      Graham Hill won 22nd Grand Prix de Monte Carlo (May 10).

      Dallas Long set world shot-put record of 66'3 1/2'' (May 29) at SPAAU Meet, Occidental College, California.

      Longest major league game in history (elapsed time) was played at Shea Stadium, N.Y. between N.Y. Mets and S.F. Giants — 7 hours and 23 minutes (May 31), 23 innings.

      A.J. Foyt of Texas won (May 30) the 500-mile Indianapolis auto-racing classic. The 29-tear-old Texan averaged 147.35 miles-per-hour to set a new record,and win a purse of $160,000.

OBITUARIES

Lady Nancy Astor, 84, an American-born woman who became internationally famous as a member of Britain's House of Commons and leader of the Cliveden Set which was alleged to favor appeasement of Nazi Germany prior to World War II. (May 2)

Carol Haney, dancing star of Broadway and Hollywood, at the age of 39. (May 11)

Leo Szilard, 66, nuclear physicist who played a major role in the development of the atom bomb. (May 30)

Jawarhalal Nehru, for 17 years Prime Minister of India, died at the age of 74. (May 27)

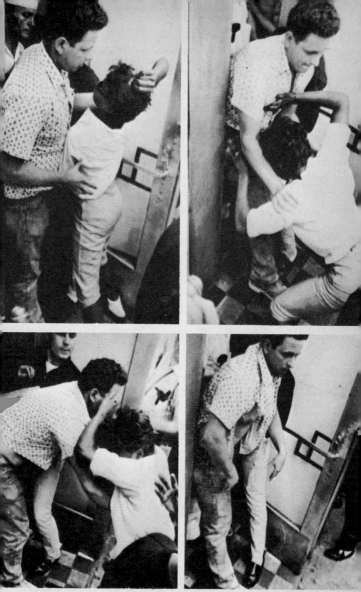

5/6/64 — Attempt to integrate downtown Nashville (Tenn.) restaurant resulted in a brief scuffle when white men barred way to Negro girl. Men stood firm, but girl didn't yield without struggle, left one man's shirt almost in tatters (bottom right).

NATIONAL NEWS

5/4/64 — Astronaut John Glenn and wife Annie in Seabrook, Texas home on day before Ohio Senatorial primary election, in which Glenn was to have run. Head injury sustained in fall forced his withdrawal from race, but his name still appeared on ballot. Next day over 200,000 Ohioans still voted to give Glenn Democratic nomination, but Senator Stephen Young easily won.

5/6/64 — Policeman turns dog loose on Negro striker in Suffolk, Va. More than 1,000 workers, predominantly Negro, protested against "segregation wages" at peanut processing plant; prostrated themselves on railroad tracks to prevent loaded boxcars from leaving. Six were hurt, 15 were arrested.

5/12/64 — Mrs. Gloria Richardson (center) with 12 other Negro demonstrators arrested in Cambridge, Md., after 300 marched in protest against appearance of Alabama Governor George Wallace. Fifty state troopers, 400 National Guardsmen were on hand to protect Wallace.

5/11/64 — First public showing of controversial experimental aircraft, the XB70 (Valkyrie), draws hundreds of visitors at North American Aviation plant in Palmdale, Cal. Craft is designed for 2,000 mph.

5/12/64 — Aviatrix Joan Merriam, 27, is greeted at Oakland after completing her eight-week, around-the-world solo flight in twin-engined Piper Apache. She flew last 150 miles on one engine.

5/13/64 — Investigators probing week-old wreckage of Pacific Airlines F-27 which crashed near Danville, Calif., discovered apparent bullet hole in cockpit bulkhead behind pilot's seat. Recently-fired gun was found in debris, while replay of control tower tapes seemed to confirm fact a passenger shot both pilot and co-pilot.

5/13/64 — Air Force F-105 jet fighter, with student pilot at controls, crashed and exploded in midst of housing development in North Las Vegas, Calif., just 1,000 feet short of the desert. Seven persons, including the pilot and four children, were killed. Aerial photo shows scene.

5/14/64 — Third straight night of violence in Cambridge, Md., following visit by Alabama Governor George Wallace, saw National Guardsmen threaten brick-throwing Negroes with bayonets.

5/18/64 — Famed flyer Jacqueline Cochran climbs from cockpit of Lockheed F-104G Super Starfighter after cracking her own speed record at Edwards Air Force Base, Calif. She averaged 1,429.297 mph, twice the speed of sound, faster than any other woman.

5/20/64—One-third scale model of two-seater Gemini capsule drops from 11,000 feet in successful test of controllable landing device called "Parasail," designed to permit astronauts to land on land instead of water.

5/14/64—Mr. and Mrs. Charles Cutler, 74 and 68 respectively, have lived for 50 years on Mrs. LBJ's Alabama farm land. They are quite satisfied with their house, but would like First Lady to fix leaky roof.

5/21/64—Malcolm X. Negro leader, returns from tour of Holy Land. His daughter, Ilysah, met him at airport.

/23/64—CORE picket con-
rolled by S.F. policeman as
undreds swarmed around
ank of America protesting
iring policies.

5/25/64 – Warren Shinsheimer, 37 year-old New York attorney and head of national "draft Scranton" movement, predicts in Washington that victory by Governor Rockefeller in June 2 California primary will give Republican Presidential nomination to Governor Scranton "no later than fourth ballot." Rockefeller won in Oregon

5/28/64 – Volunteer vigilantes, organized by Orthodox Jewish sect in Brooklyn, move through alley on night patrol. They hope to prevent trouble, protect citizens in crime-ridden area. Three nights later, teacher was raped, fatally stabbed.

5/31/64 – Seaboard Railway's "Silver Meteor" rocketed off rails in Allendale, S.C. 400 passengers were aboard New York-bound train; 51 were seriously injured.

NATIONAL NEWS-END

LIMA SOCCER DISASTER

5/25/64 — Irate fans chasing soccer referee across field at National Stadium in Lima, Peru marked start of one of sport's most tragic riots. Incident occurred in Olympic qualifying game between Argentina and Peru. Visitors led 1-0, when, with minutes left in game, Peru tied the score. Referee nullified the score for rules violation, and 45,000 highly-emotional Peruvian spectators protested violently. Bottles and other objects were hurled at the referee and a few fans (as the one above) climbed fence separating stands from field. More followed and soon crowd became a mob, started to tear down the fence. Then the police moved in.

5/25/64 — Having been caught short-handed in violent soccer riot two months before, Lima police were ready this time. Using clubs, police dogs for protection, they hurled tear-gas grenades into the tightly-packed stands. Crowd panicked. (See next page.)

5/25/64 — Frantic fans in Lima's National Stadium jammed into exit tunnels to escape tear gas (top photo, opposite page). Since game was not yet over, passage was blocked by iron gates. Force of mob finally broke gates and spectators scrambled madly over one another to get out. Total of 218 of them never made it; their bodies were lined up that night in Lima Hospital (second photo); thousands turned out for mass burial (bottom photo). Father holds lifeless form of son (below).

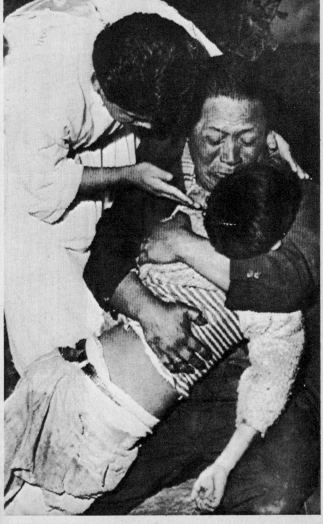

5/1/64 — Primier Fidel Castro links arms with brother Raul (left) and Cuban President Osvaldo Dorticos in Havana's May Day parade, an annual Communist event. Champion sugar cane cutter trails (white hat). Cuba's sugar crop is so low, Castro is hard-pressed to meet Iron Curtain commitments.

5/6/64 — Writhing Australian university student is dragged from U.S. Consulate grounds during racial segregation protest in Sydney. Hundreds of students rallied opposite Consulate, burned cross on the grounds. Australia itself has immigration policy aimed to exclude Negroes.

5/6/64 — U.S. resumes relations with Panama as Ambassador Jack Hood Vaughn (center) arrives in Panama City to present credentials at Presidential Palace.

5/1/64 — Moscow May Day parade revealed for first time new twin rockets, which are ground-to-air missiles that are carried in pairs on self-propelled launchers. They were part of rocket power display in Red Square.

ASWAN DAM

5/9/64 — Egyptian girl throws herself on hood of car carrying President Nasser and Russian Premier Nikita Khrushchev in Cairo. Security arrangements broke down repeatedly as large crowds turned out for Soviet leader's visit to inaugurate the Aswan Dam.

5/14/64 — Sand barrier is dynamited (above), diverting Nile River through six giant tunnels at Aswan Dam. President Nasser and Premier Khrushchev set off explosion by pushbutton. Project will bring new electric power, additional cropland to Egypt. Nasser originally planned to pay for project when he nationalized Suez Canal (see map) in 1956. In end, he had to seek other funds; Russians gave him 12-year, $271 million loan for Dam.

5/9/64 — Body of Ngo Dinh Can, youngest brother of the late Vietnamese President Ngo Dinh Diem, is untied from pole following his execution in Saigon. Original execution order called for him to be beheaded, but it was altered without explanation, and he was shot. Blood can be seen on his white trousers. His brother was assassinated during overthrow of his government last year.

5/11/64 — Heavy guard watches over handcuffed Alberto Natin (right) as he met some 13,000 creditors in Buenos Aires stadium to explain his repayment plan of a $14.4 million loss by finance company that he headed.

5/13/64 — Police carry struggling anti-apartheid demonstrator from Oslo tennis stadium during Norway-South Africa Davis Cup matches. Police arrested 20 protesting S. African racism.

5/15/64 — Mafia leader Luciano Liggio — "the most wanted man in Sicily" — is carried on a stretcher after arrest in Palermo. Crippled by spinal tuberculosis, Liggio, 38, who defied capture for 16 years, was found helpless in bed, too sick to resist arrest. One of his own men informed.

5/16/64 — Fireman covers himself with blanket in Caracas during Venezuela's worst fire. Five factories were destroyed, damage ran to $22 million. President Raul Leoni ordered full investigation.

S.S. POMONA

5/18/64—A hawsehole view of the body of Jack Natvig, 51, being removed from his room on Brazilian owned SS *Pomona* to the Honolulu morgue where an autopsy will be performed. The Norwegian skipper was slain with an axe aboard ship on high seas 5/15. The word "KILL", crudely painted on forecastle bulkhead of the *Pomona* was discovered at dawn 5/19 adding to the mystery surrounding the murder since the chief suspect was locked in an isolation cell when painting was done.

5/19/—Norwegian consular representative Torkel Westly (R) interviews Chief Mate Al Olsen (second from R). Joining in interview are Capt. E. D. Hassall (L) of ship's agent, Theodore H. Davies, Ltd., and Alan C. Wheeler, senior agent for firm.

5/23/64—U. S. Marshall Wesley Petrie (R), serves notice of seizure on Pomona's acting captain, Alf Olsen. Order was issued by U. S. District Court judge after two crew members filed damage suits against owners.

5/19/64 — World heavyweight boxing champion Cassius Clay (right) sports native "kente" robe as he is greeted by Ghana President Kwame Nkrumah in Accra. On extended tour of Africa and the Mid-East, Clay irritated hosts in Nigeria by cutting short his visit.

5/19/64 — United States uncovered network of more than 40 microphones secreted deep in walls of U.S. Embassy in Moscow, presumably planted there some 11 years ago. An undisclosed number were still in working condition. Photo at right shows side view of microphone with probe tube attached. Lower photo shows placement in wall, with tube leading from surface of wall to microphone embedded further back. U.S. filed protest note. Tip from Soviet defector led to discovery.

5/21/64 — Injured woman, shot during clash between East Indians and Negroes, is carried to hospital in British Guiana. Dispute stems from 102-day-old strike by East Indian sugar workers, supported by Premier Cheddi Jagan. Not even reinforced British troops could halt violence.

5/26/64 — Despite fog, Russian sailors engage in impromptu dance to celebrate 20th anniversary of Russian victory against German armies at Sevastopol during World War II. Photo is one of the first ever taken by Westerner in Crimea, normally closed to foreigners.

5/26/64 — U.N. Secretary-General U Thant tells newsmen anyone suggesting use of an atomic bomb in Southeast Asia is "out of his mind." He mentioned no names but reference to Sen. Barry Goldwater was unmistakable.

5/27/64 — Members of British Army mortar crew duck as they fire at rebel tribes during skirmish in Radfan Mountains of Federation of South Arabia

ADEN - YEMEN

5/13/64 — When quantities of Soviet-made arms began slipping across border from Yemen to dissident tribesmen, known as "Red Wolves," in Federation of South Arabia, British Army forces acted, bombed border fortress. Yemen complained to U.N., which condemned British action despite charge that Egyptian army garrison in Yemen was supplying arms. Federation is a British protectorate on southern tip of Arabian peninsula, contains port and military base of Aden, Britain's sea link with the Far East and last major military staging area in Middle East.

5/13/64 — Tribesmen loyal to Federation outside fortress at Thumier. It houses operations center for Arab-British forces engaged in putting down rebels. Region is just 60 miles north of Aden.

5/5/64 — Yemen-based guerilla fighter (opposite page) attends anti-Royalist meeting in Taiz, Yemen. Tribesman crossed into Federation of South Arabia, captured, killed two British soldiers (inserts), paraded their heads on poles in Taiz. Below, British paratroopers advance across rock-strewn terrain near border.

5/7/64— Bare-chested British soldier guards supply caravan moving up to mountain fortress near Federation's border with Yemen. Camel carries water cans, carton of beer. Most of Federation's 660,000 Arabs live on the one percent of the land that can be cultivated. Rest of country is harsh land of desert and rock.

5/27/64 — Indian Prime Minister Jawaharlal Nehru (inset) died of heart attack in New Delhi at age 74. Next day, Nehru, though an agnostic, was committed to Hindu funeral pyre, ignited by grandson. Four died in crush of huge, emotional crowd. Born into wealthy family, Nehru was educated in England. At 30, he became follower of Mahatma Gandhi; worked for Indian independence, spent 10 years in British jails. His nation's leader 17 years, Nehru advocated neutrality

INTERNATIONAL NEWS-END

ENTERTAINMENT, SPORTS & THE ARTS

INDIANAPOLIS

5/13/64 — As his right front tire careens toward stands at left, veteran driver Paul Russo controls car during trial run for Indianapolis 500-Mile race.

5/30/64 — On big day, rookie driver Dave MacDonald skids coming out of fourth turn on just second lap of race. Right behind him in car 25 is popular Eddie Sachs.

5/30/64 — Impact of MacDonald-Sachs collision hurls debris outward; fuel ignites.

5/30/64 — Within seconds huge fireball mushrooms from track. Five other cars piled up. Sachs was killed; MacDonald was critically injured, died soon after.

5/30/64 — Smoke, fire, debris halted race two hours. After restart, defending champion Parnelli Jones gained lead, made pit stop on 55th lap only to have spark ignite gas tank. Jones saved himself by timely leap from car (below). A.J. Foyt (insert), the 1961 champ, went on to win, setting record of 147.350 mph.

5/24/64 — Canadian-bred Northern Dancer (7) thrusts nose across finish line, a full neck ahead of Hill Rise in 90th running of Kentucky Derby. Bill Hartack rode winner which set new record for 1 1/4-mile distance of two minutes flat.

5/27/64 – Fingers crossed behind her, Mrs. Donald Campbell watches her husband flash past in his Bluebird racing car. He hopes to set new speed mark in South Australia.

5/6/64 — French starlet Reine Rohan arrives at Cannes Film Festival in eye-popping gown. Photographers, used to attention-getting outfits at annual cinema event, all but blew their bulbs.

5/8/64 — After five weeks in hospital following near-fatal heart attack, actor Peter Sellers receives warm homecoming from his wife, Swedish actress Britt Eklund, in Beverly Hills. Sellers faces extended recuperation period of possibly two more months.

5/12/64 — TV comedian Steve Allen waves from perch atop a 1916 "Flying Jennie" bi-plane. Stunt was for his television show. Said Steve upon landing: "It's great for the sinuses."

5/14/64 — Ten years after snapping foot-racing's most formidable barrier —the four-minute mile—Dr. Roger Bannister, (center) celebrates anniversary of event with men who paced him, Chris Brasher (left) and Chris Chataway, in London. Bottom photo shows trio in same order after Bannister ran·3:59.4 at Oxford. Time has since been bettered many times; record is 3:54.4.

5/25/64 — Mary Tyler Moore, TV wife of Dick Van Dyke, gets off-video kiss from Dick after they both won Emmy awards in Hollywood for their performances in a continuing series.

5/31/64 — Matador Pepe Osuna, thrown to ground by bull moments before, kneels and taunts beast as blood streams down his face in Tiajuana. He later killed bull.

5/9/64 — Jim Measures of Widnes team slams Peter Flanagan of Rovers to ground in Rugby Cup finals in London. Widnes won.

5/25/64 — Actress Elizabeth Taylor plants kiss on actor Hume Cronyn after presenting him with a Tony Award for supporting role in "Hamlet", her hubby stars.

ENTERTAINMENT, SPORTS & THE ARTS–END

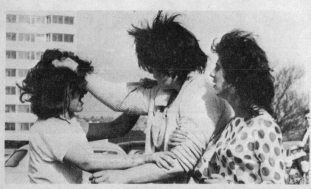

5/17/64 — Two teenage girls begin tussling as violence erupts between rival gangs— the "Mods" and the "Rockers"—at English sea resort. Police arrested 40 youths.

5/15/64 — As boy looks on in horror. Mark Flagge lies on pavement after being knocked 20 feet by car while getting off school bus. He is expected to recover.

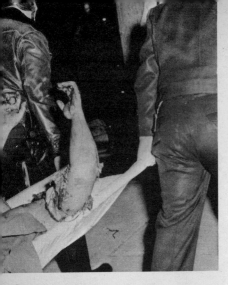

5/23/64 – Fire victim, his arms severely burned, is carried from All Hallows Church in San Francisco after blaze raced through Roman Catholic parish hall, killing six and injuring 70 others. Some 300 partygoers were thrown into panic when torch being used in Tahitian fire dance touched curtain, sent building up in flames.

5/27/64 – Lady lion tamer Rita Florian coaxes lion (left) into cage (right) in Cantania, Sicily. Four of her lions escaped, spread fear and panic in city streets. Machinegun wielding policemen covered her as she went about perilous task. She and beasts are with visiting African circus.

5/12/64 – Big business got full treatment from small stockholder when Wilma Soss showed up at New York Central System's annual meeting in Chicago. She is head of Federation of Women Stockholders, came to meeting in Chinese pajamas, a lace mantilla, and carried a battery-powered bull horn to enable her to be heard. As for shoes, she brought them along, soon removed them.

MAY – END

SUMMARY-JUNE 1964

NATIONAL

The U.S. will permit an iron curtain country, Rumania, to buy most of the commodities which are sold to free-world countries including industrial plants and possibly a nuclear reactor.

Senator Barry Goldwater of Arizona became an overwhelming favorite to capture the Republican nomination for President by defeating Governor Nelson Rockefeller of New York in the California primary (June 2)...... In the same primary elections, **Pierre Salinger**, former press Secretary to Presidents John F. Kennedy and Lyndon B. Johnson, won the Democratic nomination for Senator...... In New York, two long-time Democratic political bosses went down to defeat. In the Bronx, **Charles Buckley**, a Congressman for 30 years, lost to reform candidate Jonathan Bingham, and former Tammany chief **Carmine de Sapio** was beaten in a comeback attempt by Edward Koch...... **Governor George Wallace** of Alabama said (June 7) that he would place his name on the ballot as a Presidential candidate in as many states as possible. He said he expected to win 70 electoral votes as an anti-civil rights candidate...... Former Vice-President **Richard Nixon** urged Governor Romney to fight Senator Goldwater for the Republican nomination...... **Governor William W. Scranton** of Pennsylvania became Senator Goldwater's leading rival for the Republican nomination when he declared himself a candidate at the Maryland Republican Convention (June 12)...... a group of Republican faculty members of Harvard, Tufts and M.I.T. predicted that if Goldwater ran he would lose every state...... **Governor Rockefeller** withdrew (June 15) as a presidential aspirant in favor of Governor Scranton...... **Henry Cabot Lodge** resigned (June 23) as U.S. Ambassador to S. Viet Nam to help Governor Scranton's campaign for the Republican Presidential nomination. Lodge was succeeded by **General Maxwell Taylor**, Chairman of the Joint Chiefs of Staff. General Taylor was replaced by Lt. General **Earle G. Wheeler** who was promoted over four 4-star Generals...... **Attorney General Robert Kennedy** announced (June 23) that he would not be a candidate for the Democratic Senatorial nomination in New York.

A strike by **Actors Equity**, trade union of the New York theatre, was settled after one day. Only two shows missed performances during the brief walk-out.

Police Commissioner Michael Murphy of New York City said (June 8) he did not expect racial friction in the city to explode into violence during the summer...... **Martin Luther King** and 17 others were arrested (June 11) for trying to eat in a segregated restaurant in St. Augustine, Florida. A Federal judge ordered (June 22) the Governor of Florida to show cause why he should not be held in contempt for barring civil rights demonstrations in **St. Augustine**. Negroes in the community were attacked (June 26) by 800 white terrorists. Nineteen persons were injured. Police arrested several whites but freed them in the face of threats by the mob.

Two white civil rights workers from New York and a Negro from Mississippi were reported missing (June 22) in that state shortly after being released from jail where they had been held for a few hours on a speeding charge. They were Andrew Goodman, 20, and Michael Schwerner, 26, of New York and James Cheney, 21. Their station wagon was discovered burned outside Philadelphia, Miss.

The U.S. Senate voted the first cloture in a civil rights debate 71-29 following the longest filibuster since 1917. On the 83rd day of the debate, the Senate finally passed the bill (June 19) by a vote of 73 to 27. Senator Goldwater voted against the bill and was denounced by Senator Everett Dirksen, Republican leader of the Senate...... Malcolm X branded civil rights bill a "rubber check which will build up Negroes for a big let-down because it cannot be cashed." On the other hand, Roy Wilkins of NAACP described the bill as "giant step forward for Negroes."

The U.S. Supreme Court ruled that the Communist Party need not register its membership with the Department of Justice...... In another decision the Court ruled (June 15) that both houses of state legislatures must be apportioned on the basis of population. The Court also ruled that evidence obtained by state courts from witnesses forced to waive their rights under the 5th Amendment by a grant of immunity could not be used against them in a Federal court.

The Attorney General of New York State proposed that New York theatres charge $25 a ticket for the best seats as a means of balking ticket scalpers.

The House of Representatives voted to raise the pay of 1.7 million Federal employees. At the same time they voted themselves a raise from $22,500 a year to $30,000 a year.

The Federal Trade Commission (FTC) ordered cigarette manufacturers to prepare to include on their packages by 1965 a warning that cigarettes may cause death from cancer and other diseases.

Property damage estimated at $20 million and 24 deaths resulted from floods in Montana.

INTERNATIONAL

The ruling Congress Party of India elected (June 1) Lal Bahardur Shastri, 59, to succeed the deceased Nehru as Prime Minister.

Martial law was declared (June 3) in Seoul, capital of S. Korea, as 10,000 students rioted against the government. The rioting spread to ten other cities and quieted only after President Chung Hee Park announced that 576 government officials would be fired.

U.S. planes attacked pro-communist gun emplacements in Laos. Flights were temporarily suspended (June 10) at the request of neutralist Prime Minister Souvanna Phouma but resumed (June 12) with Phouma's approval ..... The U.S. warned Red China that it was ready to go to war to defend independent Laos and S. Viet Nam.

Congo Prime Minister Cyrille Adoula asked the United Nations (June 1) to suppress a rebellion in Kiwi Province. The rebels captured Albertville, capital of North Katanga.

The U.N. Security Council voted (June 20) to leave its peace-keeping force on Cyprus three more months, until September 26.

The left-center government of Aldo Moro resigned in Italy when a dispute over aid to church schools split the coalition.

Pope Paul VI told a gathering of 26 cardinals that the Roman Catholic Church was giving "wide and profound study to birth control."

The U.S. and the Soviet signed (June 1) a Soviet-American Consular Agreement, theoretically giving U.S. officials prompt access to any U.S. citizen detained or arrested in USSR.

SPORTS

Sandy Koufax of the Los Angeles Dodgers tied a record held by three other pitchers by pitching the third no-hitter of his career to beat the Philadelphia Phillies 3-0 (June 4)...... A perfect game, first in modern National League history, was pitched (June 20) by Jim Bunning of the Phillies in beating the New York Mets 6-0.

Northern Dancer, winner of the Derby and Preakness, failed to complete the triple crown when he ran third to Quadrangle in the Belmont Stakes (June 5).

"Champagne" Tony Lema beat out Mike Souchak in the $50,000 Thunderbird Golf Tournament by one stroke with a score of 276. Ken Venturi won the U.S. Open Golf Tournament with a score of 278.

OBITUARIES

William Maxwell Aitken, Lord Beaverbrook, 85, a Canadian who built a newspaper empire in England (June 9).

NATIONAL NEWS

6/11/64 — Rev. King peers between bars of his jail cell after being arrested on charges of trespassing at motel. He permitted himself to be arrested to dramatize civil rights struggle. In Jacksonville, Federal Judge Bryan Simpson said St. Augustine officials were trying to break integration movement through "cruel and inhuman punishment" of prisoners.

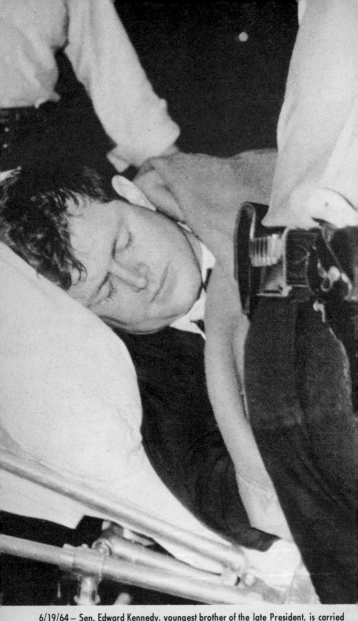

6/19/64 — Sen. Edward Kennedy, youngest brother of the late President, is carried into Southampton, Mass., hospital following crash of private plane .(See page 163.)

6/9/64 – Whirlwind round of speeches and public appearances momentarily catches up to President Lyndon B. Johnson at commencement exercises at Pennsylvania's Swarthmore College. He told graduates that those who felt strong Federal government was a threat to individual liberty were stating "phantom fears." He said: "The truth is – far from crushing the individual – government at its best liberates him from the enslaving forces of his environment." Two days later he spoke at Holy Cross College, expressed his hopes for the "Great Society," said that recent "breakthrough" meant that "long promised day of economical nuclear power is close at hand."

6/1/64 – Israel's Prime Minister Levi Eshkol is greeted with full military honors at White House by President and Mrs. Johnson. Mrs. Eshkol is at right. Visit was first ever to U. S. by an Israeli chief of government.

6/9/64 – Helmeted police round up demonstrators at Tuscaloosa, Ala., church. City officials banned street demonstrations, but 500 Negroes defied restriction, then sought refuge in church; hurled bottles, rocks at police. Latter surrounded church, lobbed tear gas shells in windows, arrested 60.

6/10/64 – Anthony R. Accardo, Jr., adopted son of Anthony (Big Tuna) Accardo, reputed crime syndicate head, leaves Chicago church with bride, Janet Hawley, former Miss Utah. Underworld figures, FBI agents attended.

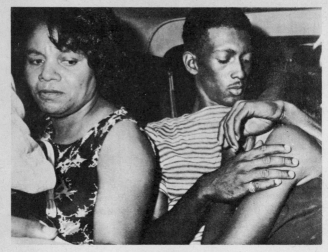

6/10/64 — Integration marches in St. Augustine, Fla., the oldest city in the U. S., touched off three weeks of violence as organized white segregationists resorted to force to intimidate demonstrators. City officials hoped to avoid incidents by banning night demonstrations by civil rights workers, but Federal Judge issued order enjoining them from enforcing ban. Above, Negro youth comforts injured girl on way to hospital after whites attacked marchers.

6/10/64 — Boston University chaplain William England holds head in pain, is led to safety by Negro girl after whites broke up civil rights march in St. Augustine, Fla. Opposite page, blood-spattered Negroes confer after being attacked.

6/10/64— Ivory Ward sits behind bullet-shattered windshield of his small car in St. Augustine. White youths fired at vehicle, narrowly missed him.

6/11/64 — Monson Motel in St. Augustine was focal point of integration efforts. Here, manager James Brock (center) grimaces as he turns away Rev. Martin Luther King (right) and Rev. Ralph Abernathy from motel restaurant. King, 17 others were jailed.

6/14/64 — Despite King's arrest, previous violence, demonstrations go on as Negroes seek service at motel restaurant. Manager Brock, locked door of restaurant, sits in office (left) while Negroes congregate outside, led by Rev. Lavert Taylor (holding book). Police arrested entire group, numbering 30. Meanwhile, in Washington, Senate neared vote on civil rights bill.

6/15/64 — Former major-league baseball star Jackie Robinson taps foot in time to music as "Freedom Marchers" choir from North Carolina sings for mass meeting in St. Augustine. He came to city to support the integration movement.

6/16/64 — Ku Klux Klan attorney J. B. Stoner of Atlanta (right) and St. Augustine white supremacy leader Halstead Muncey confer prior to talking to newsmen. They said violence would continue as long as Negroes continued to "invade" white areas of the nation's oldest city.

6/18/64 — Motel manager Brock (left) forcibly ejects one of several Jewish rabbis who followed Negro integrationists to motel parking lot for prayer meeting. Entire group was arrested before the service could be conducted. Action occurred day before the Senate passed civil rights bill. Incident was just start of the day for the motel manager (see below).

6/18/64 — In premature test of civil rights bill's public accommodations section, five Negroes, two whites dived into motel swimming pool. Brock reacted by hurling two jugs of muriatic acid (a cleansing agent) into pool. When demonstrators failed to leave, police moved in. One stripped off his socks, shoes, dived into pool and began to pummel swimmers, who did not resist. White crowd looked on, jeering. After pool scuffle was over, police arrested 34 demonstrators.

6/22/64 — Scene of protests switched to public beach in St. Augustine, where white reaction erupted with new fury. On first day, mobs of club-wielding whites (above) beat Negroes who showed up on beach. Police broke up fighting, arrested members of both groups. Two days later (below), police protected Negroes on beach, but whites waited in surf, attacked Negroes when they entered the water.

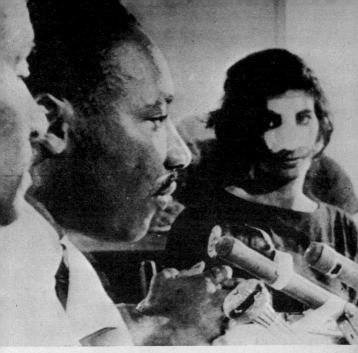

6/24/64 — Rev. King announces plans for renewed integration efforts, despite what he called "reign of terror" by segregationists. He called for Federal protection. Looking on at right is Elaine Evans, who had nose broken in recent demonstration.

6/25/64 — State troopers, acting for first time under orders to quell white violence, clubbed boy on beach. City moved to establish bi-racial committee.

6/11/64 — Cleveland Donald Jr. (right) is accompanied by attorney Derrick Bell as he arrives to register at all-white U. of Mississippi in Oxford. Federal court ordered his admission, which was accomplished without incident.

6/14/64 — Rev. William DuBay, who wrote to the Pope asking removal of James Francis Cardinal McIntyre for failure to take strong civil rights stand, waves from in front of his predominantly all-Negro parish in Compton, Calif. Father DuBay was relieved of his duties, later altered his stand.

6/21/64 — Dr. Leonard Marmor of UCLA points to arm of Mrs. Blanche Sheets of Los Angeles where a section of nerve, taken from another human, was grafted into her wrist. Disclosure of operation, first successful nerve graft between humans, was made at opening of AMA convention in San Francisco.

6/18/64 — Development of new "duplex" rifle cartridge by Army is revealed in Washington. Bullet, designed to be used by standard rifles employed by NATO forces, is piggyback affair with one bullet fitting into back of other. Upon firing, they will separate, increasing the strike area.

6/16/64 — Six persons died when bus plunged through gaping hole in Lake Pontchartrain Causeway near New Orleans. Barge created break when it rammed into the span. Two aboard bus escaped with injuries.

6/21/64 — Rev. Martin Luther King addresses huge crowd of over 70,000 in Chicago's Soldier Field at civil rights rally. He told throng that seven southern cities, including Birmingham and St. Augustine, would be testing grounds for civil rights bill.

MISSISSIPPI

6/21/64 — Three civil rights workers— (left to right) Michael Schwerner, 24; Negro James Chaney, 21; and Andrew Goodman, 20 — were reported missing in Mississippi. Three were part of group seeking to aid Negro voter registration in state. Chaney was born, raised in Miss. Other two were New Yorkers.

6/23/64 — Following tip, police found station wagon in which three were last seen. They had been arrested for speeding, were released after paying fine. Found near Philadelphia, Miss., car was gutted by fire. As apprehension mounted for safety of trio, Attorney General Robert Kennedy ordered FBI into the investigation.

6/24/64 — Former CIA Director Allen Dulles (right) confers with Miss. Gov. Paul Johnson as part of fact-finding trip ordered by President Johnson. After one day of conferences, Dulles reported "a very real" law enforcement problem existed in the state.

6/25/64 — Parents of two missing white civil rights workers from New York tell press, television their sons were devoted to work "which should be task of every American." Mother of third youth, James Chaney, joined news conference, via phone-hookup from Miss.

6/25/64 — U. S. sailors (left) join in search for missing civil rights workers on direct orders from President Johnson. They searched swamps, woods in Neshoba County, while, below, FBI agents in boats, supplied by Miss. State Game and Fishing Commission, begin to drag the Pearl River.

6/29/64 — Mrs. Michael Schwerner, wife of missing civil rights worker, and Congressman Ogden Reid talk with reporters after meeting with President Johnson. She and her husband had been active in civil rights movement for two years, established Negro community center in Meridian, Miss. last January. At month's end there was still no trace of the missing men.

6/19/64 — While CAA inspector and State trooper look over wreckage of plane in which Sen. Edward Kennedy was injured (and two others died), his wife Joan (insert) stands vigil in Mass. hospital. Though severely injured, he will recover.

6/22/64 — President Johnson greets Turkish Premier Ismet Inonu after latter landed in helicopter on White House lawn after trip from Williamsburg, Va. The two will discuss ways of averting war between Greece and Turkey over Cyprus issue.

6/29/64 — Pennsylvania Gov. William Scranton shakes hands with well-wishers, many of whom hold Goldwater placards, in downtown Atlanta, Ga. Scranton, after long delay, entered race for Republican presidential nomination two weeks ago.

6/30/64 — Spectacular two-plane collision is photographed over the Atlantic as two U. S. Air Force planes, practicing para-medic astronaut recovery operations, ram into each other. Seven were rescued, an equal number killed. Ten were missing.

6/27/64 — Margaret Ann Goldwater Holt, daughter of Sen. Barry Goldwater, helps her bridegroom Richard in helicopter, following wedding reception in Phoenix.

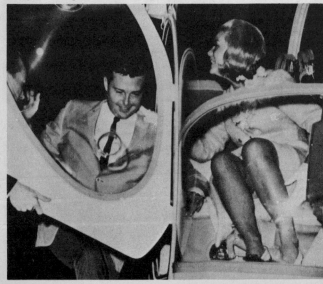

6/4/64 — Mother and child rest and eat at refugee camp in Vientiane ,Laos, after fleeing from their homes in North Laos following take-over of Plaine Des Jarres by Communist Pathet Lao forces. Refugees sorely lack food, clothing.

6/3/64 — Swedish Princess Margaretha, 29, prepares to sunbathe on steps of Haga Castle in Stockholm. She is engaged to marry a British businessman this month.

6/4/64 — Horst Adolf Eichmann, 24-year-old second son of former Nazi SS officer, Adolf Eichmann, who was executed in Israel, walks to his home in San Fernando, Argentina after holding press conference, in which he praised father as a "martyr."

6/6/64 — Two decades after history's largest sea-air invasion took place on the beaches of Normandy in France (bottom photo), youngsters search out shells in sand, while beachfront itself sports cabanas, instead of fortifications. In moving television interview, Gen. Dwight D. Eisenhower, recalling D-Day, said: "Everything was going wrong that could go wrong. Finally the thing that pulled this out was the bravery and the courage and the initiative of the American G. I. That's what did it."

6/8/64 — Urn containing ashes of India's late Prime Minister Nehru is carried by his grandsons Rajiv (left) and Sanjaya during funeral procession at Allahabad, Nehru's birthplace. Following Nehru's request, a handful of ashes were thrown into the Ganges, remainder were scattered from an airplane. Thousands surged into river; one woman drowned.

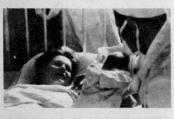

6/8/64 — Soviet Cosmonauts Valentina Tereshkova Nikolayev and her husband Andrian admire their first child, a daughter, born in Moscow. Child is first ever born to parents who have flown in space. He made 94 orbits in '62; she circled earth 48 times following year, becoming first woman to venture into outer space.

6/10/64 — India's new Prime Minister Lal Bahadur Shastri faces first press conference after his unanimous election in New Delhi to succeed Nehru. Only five feet tall, he will lead nation of 450 million, one-seventh the earth's population.

6/10/64 – SS "Pomona", known as "death ship" after her captain was murdered at sea last month, is shown leaving Honolulu for Formosa with a Chinese crew under Norwegian officers. One day out, she was reported afire and most of the crew was ordered into lifeboats, picked up safely. Fire was later brought under control.

6/10/64 – German woman looks up from work in fields to stare at sky as paratroopers of U. S. Army units descend near UM as part of the largest post-war maneuvers held in Germany. One division, three battalions are involved.

6/15/64 – French troops embark for home at port of Algiers. They are last French army units to leave Algeria which is now an independent nation. Departure was hailed by Algerian President Ben Bella as an "important event" which "consolidates our independence." French colonized country 134 years ago.

6/16/64 – Two four-story apartment buildings are toppled by earthquake in Niigata, Japan. Damage was estimated at $1 billion, but, despite fact tremor was only slightly less than the destructive 1923 quake, which killed over 140,000, only 24 persons lost their lives.

6/22/64 — Dr. Otto Hahn, 85-year-old Nobel Prize-winning nuclear scientist, is caught in reflective mood after launching of world's second nuclear-powered ship, named for him, at Kiel, West Germany. The 15,000-ton ship cost $13.2 million. It was built by two West German firms, has a 100,000-horse power reactor.

6/22/64 — Perspiring soldier stands guard as Dr. Francois (Papa Doc) Duvalier makes speech after having taken oath as life-term president of Haiti in Port Au Prince. Often accused of using terrorism and even practicing voodoo to keep nation's 4.5 million population in line, Duvalier held referendum on his right to be president for life, announced he had won eight hours before polls closed. In speech he pledged total dedication of his life to his people.

6/24/64 — Cuban Professor Juan Alvarez, 40, and his wife Hilda talk to reporters after asking for political asylum in Ireland. Pair slipped away from crippled Cuban plane which landed at Shannon Airport. He said he would be shot within an hour if forced to return to Cuba.

6/26/64 — Former Katangese President Moise Tshombe receives hero's welcome upon return to Leopoldville in the Congo from his exile. He immediately conferred with Congo leaders on ways to stop Red revolts .

INTERNATIONAL NEWS-END

6/21/64 — Toni Lee Shelley, 19, is escorted from waters of Lake Michigan in Chicago by unidentified policeman, who waded out to make "pinch," after Miss Shelley showed up in topless bathing suit. She said she saw nothing indecent about human body. Police saw it differently, booked her for improper bathing attire.

6/1/64 — Dreamy-eyed Mick Jagger, shaggy-haired member of Rolling Stones singing group, is escorted through mob of London teen-agers by steely-eyed policeman.

6/5/64 — Los Angeles Dodger pitcher Sandy Koufax holds up three fingers to symbolize third no-hitter of his career, a 12-strikeout, near perfect (one walk), 3-0 win over the Phillies in Philadelphia. Only Bob Feller has as many in modern baseball history.

6/8/64 — British actor Stewart Granger, 51, and 22-year-old Belgian beauty queen Viviane Lecerf exchange wedding rings in civil ceremony in Geneva, Switzerland. It was third marriage for Granger.

6/12/64 — Singer Judy Garland is seen escorted by Mark Herron from Hong Kong hospital. Sources close to the singer denied reports that she and Herron had married.

6/15/64 — Academy Award-winning actress Sophia Loren strikes seductive pose on Rome set of her new film "Marriage – Italian Style." Her outfit seems certain to tempt any man into proposing.

→

6/17/64 — Welterweight champion Emile Griffith holds up two fingers, signifying his second victory over challenger Luis Rodriguez in Las Vegas. Rodriguez took title from Griffith, lost it back later, then failed to regain it in 15-round decision.

6/22/64 — Baseball's newest, and richest, bonus babies are (top) Willie Crawford, a Fremont (Cal.) High School boy, signing for $100,000 with Los Angeles Dodgers as Scout Al Campanis looks on; and (bottom) Rick Reichardt, 21-year-old U. of Wisconsin junior, who was given $125,000 by Los Angeles Angels.

6/21/64 — In New York, Phillie pitcher Jim Bunning fires last strike (against Met pinch-hitter John Stephenson) to wrap up first perfect, no-hit game pitched in National League since 1880. Father of seven, Bunning picked Father's Day to hurl his masterpiece.

6/20/64 — Ken Venturi gets hug from his wife after winning 64th National Open golf tournament at Congressional Country Club in Washington, D. C. with 278 total, second lowest in Open history. Oppressive heat almost felled Venturi on final day; doctor accompanied him over last 18 holes, fed him salt tablets. Victory was his first major tournament triumph in four years.

6/25/64 — Long-distance swimmer Britt Sullivan holds seven-month-old daughter Kim before plunging into surf at Far Rockaway, N. Y., on first leg of her proposed swim across Atlantic Ocean. Planning to swim 18 hours a day, she hoped to make England in five months, but three days later failed to keep rendezvous with supply boat, was listed as missing. The 5-5, 150-pound, 29-year-old divorcee had refused to swim in shark cage, was presumably victim of attack. Coast Guard, at first skeptical of her disappearance (she had been reported missing on other distance swims) conducted three-day search, finally listed her as lost, after finding no trace.

6/27/64 — Academy Award winner Ernest Borgnine, 47, kisses bride, Broadway musical comedy star Ethel Merman, after their wedding in Beverly Hills.

6/8/64 — French movie queen Brigitte Bardot, caught without benefit of the top of her bathing suit, beat hasty retreat when photographers appeared at St. Tropez.

ENTERTAINMENT, SPORTS & THE ARTS-END

6/23/64 — Despite fact ball whizzed by her ear, tennis line judge Mrs. Dorothy Cavis-Brown slept soundly on during match at Wimbledon, much to fans' delight.

6/19/64 — Greek soccer fans run wild during match in Athens, chanting "Peru, Peru," a grim reminder of tragic riot there last month. Supposed "indifference" of players caused fans to riot, set fires in stands, charge onto the field.

6/9/64 — Too smart for grade school, Bobby Greene, 12, who flunked out of fifth grade in Titusville, Fla., squints through microscope as Brevard Junior College president looks on. Bobby, who has I. Q. of over 200, will attend college on experimental basis. He was apparently too bored in grade school.

JUNE – END

SUMMARY-JULY 1964

NATIONAL

The **Republican convention** got under way (July 13) in San Francisco's Cow Palace. Senator Barry M. Goldwater of Arizona, easily fending off the challenge of his only serious rival, Governor William W. Scranton of Pennsylvania, was nominated as the Republican Party's presidential candidate on the first ballot with 883 votes out of the 1097 cast. **U.S. Representative William E. Miller** of Lockport, N. Y., Chairman of the Republican National Committee received the vice presidential nomination...... Nominee Goldwater stirred up a tempest in his acceptance speech when he said, **"Extremism in defense of liberty is no vice; moderation in pursuit of justice is no virtue."** Governor Nelson Rockefeller of New York called the statement "dangerous, irresponsible and frightening." Former President Dwight D. Eisenhower called for an explanation...... During the convention, a scathing letter was sent to Goldwater under Governor Scranton's signature. Governor Scranton later confessed that he had neither read nor signed the letter which had been prepared and mailed by his staff...... **Dean Burch** of Arizona, a Goldwater intimate, succeeded Representative Miller as Republican National Chairman.

Governor George C. Wallace of Alabama, who had contested a number of state primaries as an Anti-Civil Rights Democrat, withdrew (July 19) as an independent presidential candidate...... **President Lyndon B. Johnson** and Senator Goldwater agreed to avoid civil rights as a campaign issue...... President Johnson eliminated (July 30) as vice-presidential possibilities for the Democratic ticket Attorney General Robert F. Kennedy, Secretary of State Dean Rusk, Peace Corps chief Sargent Shriver, Defense Secretary Robert S. McNamara, Secretary of Agriculture Orville Freeman and U. N. Ambassador Adlai Stevenson.

Ex-Governor, Leroy Collins (Fla) appointed Director of Community Relations Service created by the new Civil Rights Act. Sen. Commerce Comm. approved nomination.

Race riots rocked New York's Harlem over the week-end of July 18 following the killing of a 15-year-old Negro boy by a police lieutenant, reportedly in self-defense. The rioting continued into the following week and spread to Brooklyn, forcing the return of Mayor Robert F. Wagner from a vacation in Spain. The following week-end, race rioting broke out in the conservative, prosperous city of **Rochester, N.Y.** Governor Rockefeller sent in the National Guard to restore order...... **Negro civil rights leaders** called for a moratorium on street demonstrations until after the national elections but James Farmer, head of CORE (Committee for Racial Equality) and John Lewis, chief of the Student Non-violent Coordinating Committee (SNCC) rejected the proposal...... **The Negro director of five Washington, D.C. vocational highschools, a**

Lt. Colonel in the U.S. Army Reserve, was shot to death (July 11) in his car on a Georgia highway while returning from summer training at Fort Benning, Ga. ......Senator **Richard B. Russell** of Georgia called on the South (July 15) to obey the Civil Rights Law...... Two hotels and one motel in Jackson, Miss. integrated peacefully in accordance with the new Civil Rights Law...... A three-judge federal court upheld (July 22) the constitutionality of the Civil Rights Law as it applies to public accommodations.

Love letters written by U.S. President Warren Gamaliel Harding (1921-23) were discovered in the files of the late Mrs. James Phillips, wife of a department store owner in Harding's home town, Marion, Ohio......**Dr. Samuel H. Sheppard,** convicted of murdering his wife in a nationally publicized trial, was released from an Ohio jail after serving 10 years of a life sentence on a ruling by a federal judge that he had been deprived of his constitutional rights during the trial...... A grand jury refused to indict **Arlene Del Fava,** 27-year-old Queens, (N.Y.) secretary, whose defense of herself with a switch-blade knife against an attempted rape became a national issue when Senator Goldwater criticized her arrest by police on charges of violating New York's concealed weapons law......**Attorney Roy M. Cohn,** chief aide to the late Senator Joseph McCarthy, was acquitted in federal court of perjury charges in connection with a 5-million dollar stock swindle......**James R. Hoffa,** Teamster Union head, was found guilty in Chicago of having conspired to misuse the union's $25 million pension fund. A few weeks earlier he had been found guilty in another indictment of conspiring to tamper with a federal jury...... **The Federal Bureau of Investigation** reported that serious crimes throughout the nation rose 10% in 1962 and were up 40% since 1958 although the population had increased only 8% in that period ......, **Automobile deaths** reached a record 504 over the July 4 holiday weekend.

The U.S. Senate voted (July 29) 388-8 to raise social security payments by 5% and added some 800,000 persons to the 20 million already eligible for social security benefits. Among the new beneficiaries are 150,000 physicians and 600,000 elderly people. ...... **The Senate** earlier (July 22) had approved a **$947.5 anti-poverty program** ...... **General Motors** reported (July 23) all-time record profits of $1,138,000,000 for the first six months of 1964.

Space craft Ranger 7 crash-landed (July 31) on the moon as planned and televised back to U.S. scientists in the Jet Propulsion Laboratory of the California Institute of Technology 4300 "close-up" pictures of the moon's surface.

INTERNATIONAL

Fidel Castro offered (July 3) to stop backing revolutionary activities in Latin America if the U.S. would end support for subversive movements in Cuba. The offer was rejected.

Red China implied (July 1) that it would fight for North Viet Nam if that country were attacked......**General Nguyen Khanh,** chief of the South Viet Nam government, called for an attack on North Viet Nam but the call was opposed by the U.S.......**General de Gaulle** proposed that the U.S., the Soviet Union, Red China and France give up all attempts to maintain zones of influence in the Indochinese Peninsula ...... The U.S. increased its forces in S. Viet Nam by 5,000, bringing the total to 21,000...... **Nyasaland** became 37th Independent African State (July 6) — The State of Malawi....... **U.S. Ambassador** to Viet Nam Maxwell D. Taylor presented credentials (July 22)...... **DeGaulle** at news conference (July 23) called on Europe to play its own independent role in world politics free from subordination to the U.S.

Khrushchev announced (July 13) a pension system which would pay 30 million Soviet farmers $112 a month. At the same time, he announced pay raises for 18 million public service workers of up to 40 per cent...... **The Chinese Reds** called K. a "capitalist"...... **Soviet industrial production** increased by 7.5% in 1963, a substantial reduction in growth rate from the previous year......**Anastas I. Mikoyan** became President of the Soviet Union succeeding Leonid I. Brezhnev who became Khrushchev's Deputy in the Communist Party Secretariat.

The Organization of American States (OAS) voted (July 25) economic and diplomatic sanctions against Cuba by a vote of 15 - 3.

Moise Tshombe became Prime Minister of the Congo. One of his first acts was to release from jail Antoine Gizenga, leader of the leftist opposition to Tshombe when the latter was Premier of the Congo's Katanga province and leader of a secessionist movement which was crushed by U.N. troops.

Aldo Moro (July 22) became Italy's Prime Minister for the second time when he formed a left-center coalition government with socialist leader Pietro Nenni as Deputy Premier. Nenni broke with the Communists after collaborating with them for ten years.

120,000 government workers walked off their jobs in Britain's first postal strike in 70 years...... **Winston Churchill,** nearly 90, made his final appearance in Britain's House of Commons.

SPORTS

Ralph Boston broke the world's record for the broad jump (July 3) with a leap of 27 feet 5 and 1/2 inches...... The U.S. inflicted a crushing defeat on Soviet athletes (July 26) in a track meet by scoring **139 points to the Soviets' 97.** U.S. men beat their Soviet rivals by the lopsided score of 91-38 while U.S. women for the first time came close to victory against Soviet women with a 48-59 point score...... **Fred Hansen** established a new world's record for the pole vault with a jump of 17 feet 4 inches...... **Dallas Long** put the shot 67 feet 10 inches for a new world mark.

Bobby Nichols won (July 19) the Professional Golfers Association tournament by three strokes over Arnold Palmer and Jack Nicklaus. His score of 271 was 9 under par.

Australia reinstated tennis players **Roy Emerson** and **Fred Stolle** who had been suspended since February, 1963, for defying a ban on overseas tournament play...... **National League won 35th All-Star game** played at Shea Stadium, N.Y. with Mays' base running and John Callison's home run...... **Willie Gilmore and John Farrington** of Champion Chi Bears were killed in auto accident (July 26).

OBITUARIES

Pierre Monteux, 89, symphony orchestra conductor for more than 50 years, a record for the profession. (July 1)

Maurice Thorez, for 30 years head of the French Communist Party. (July 12)

Herb Sheldon, 51, radio and TV star. (July 21)

James M. Landis, 63, adviser to three Presidents and former Dean of the Harvard Law School. (July 30)

7/21/64 — Bartender holds towel to his injured head after night of rioting in racially tense Harlem. Police stormed bar which was barricaded by rioters. Despite considerable gunfire, only five were injured, none by bullets.

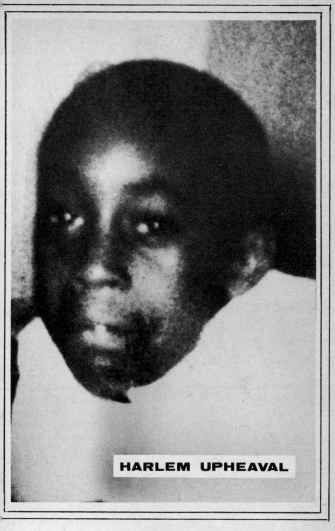

HARLEM UPHEAVAL

NATIONAL NEWS

7/16/64 — On a sunny Thursday morning on 86th St., a building superintendent allegedly squirted some Negro youths with water and a heated argument started. It ended with the death of 15-year-old James Powell (shown in 1958 photo above), shot by an off-duty New York City policeman. The city soon became a battleground.

7/16/64 — Police Lt. Thomas Gilligan, off-duty and in plain clothes, tried to stop dangerous street dispute. A boy, James Powell, 15, came at Gilligan, allegedly with knife in hand. The officer identified himself, warned the boy to halt. When Powell ignored warning, Gilligan drew his revolver, fired three times, killing Powell. Some 100 students from nearby summer school rioted in protest, bringing 100 helmeted police to the area.

7/19/64 — Street corner orators, preaching "police brutality," whipped Harlem youths into fury over the shooting, and two nights later the area erupted in mass violence. Mob leaders claimed Powell's death was deliberate murder, that any police officer should be able to disarm a boy without shooting him. Mobs sacked stores, hurled bricks, garbage, Molotov cocktails at hundreds of policemen. Responsible civil rights leaders urged crowds to stay off streets, but few listened. Youths at left used dogs for protection on second night of rioting.

7/20/64 — Mrs. Anna Powell, mother of slain boy, weeps uncontrollably as she leaves funeral home for cemetery. Meanwhile, agitators urged Harlem citizens to arm themselves for guerrilla warfare, even passed out leaflets containing directions for the making of Molotov cocktails.

7/20/64 — Negro ducks in front of automobile as helmeted police fire into air on third night of rioting. One Negro was killed as he pelted police with bricks from rooftop; 140, including 48 policemen, were injured; 520 were arrested. Property damage was extensive. Morning after (far right, opposite page), Negro surveys damage while police patrol streets.

7/30/64 — Abroad at start of riots, Mayor Robert Wagner (right) flew home, appealed to Negroes on radio-TV to cease rioting; promised that all legitimate grievances would be investigated. He met with Martin Luther King (left), who criticized New York police, then urged continuous negotiations between Negro leaders, city officials be established.

7/30/64 — King also attended meeting at N.A.A.C.P. headquarters in New York, along with other Negro leaders (left to right, Rustin, N.A.A.C.P., white attorney Jack Greenberg, Whitney Young of National Urban League, James Farmer of CORE, N.A.A.C.P. head Roy Wilkins, King, John Lewis of SNCC, A. Phillip Randolph of Negro American Labor Council, and Courtney Fox also of SNCC). They met for purpose of asking civil rights leaders to observe "broad curtailment" of mass demonstrations until after November elections, a move closely related to riots in Harlem and elsewhere, plus large civil rights demonstrations which had begun to create widespread resentment among whites. Though only 1% of Harlem citizens took part in rioting, fear of a white "backlash" against civil rights movement was aroused. Meanwhile President Johnson had ordered FBI to investigate riots to determine extent of Communist agitation.

7/20/64—New York City policemen club rioters during another bloody night. Negro leaders predicted more "hell" due to "slow-moving" grand jury investigation into shooting of Negro teenager by off duty police Lieut. night of July 16.

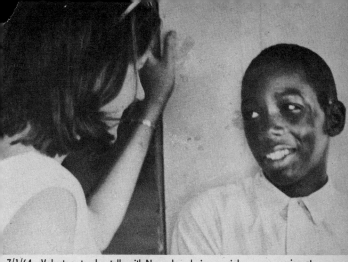

7/1/64 —Volunteer teacher talks with Negro boy during special summer session at a "freedom school" in Mississippi. Program was established on tutorial basis to improve education of Negro students, now attending segregated high schools.

7/2/64 — President Lyndon Johnson hands several pens to Attorney General Robert Kennedy after signing civil rights bill into law at White House ceremony. In address to nation, President said bill meant "the only limit to a man's hope for happiness...shall be his own ability."

7/3/64 — Following day, Negroes tested bill in Atlanta, Ga., sought admission to white restaurant. Owner Lester Maddox (at left) blocked entrance, brandished pistol at Negroes, shouted: "You ain't never gonna eat here." When Negroes persisted, Maddox, white patrons chased them with ax-handles.

7/12/64 — Former major league baseball star Jackie Robinson (at right) and CORE director James Farmer confer before start of civil rights parade in San Francisco, protesting GOP candidacy of Senator Goldwater.

7/4/64 — Independence Day segregationist rally in Atlanta flares into violence when two Negroes, accompanied by white girl, entered grandstand. Man at right beats one Negro with chair, while second (left) flees. Police came to rescue.

7/8/64 — Three pre-dawn explosions in McComb, Miss., ripped through wall of house in which 10 civil rights workers were sleeping. Two were injured by blasts, which apparently came from home-made bombs hurled from the street.

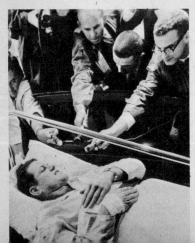

7/9/64 — Senator Edward Kennedy is questioned by newsman as he is taken from Cooley Dickinson hospital in Northampton, Mass., to be transferred to New England Baptist Hospital in Boston where he will be near his family for period of convalescence of some six to ten months. His back was broken in airplane crash last month.

EPUBLICAN NATIONAL CONVENTION

/13/64—Pennsylvania Governor
William Scranton pauses in his
ush for votes to bite into ear of
orn at meeting of Iowa delegation
utside Cow Palace in San Francis-
o, site of the Republican Party's
ational convention.

7/15/64 — Though Senator Barry Goldwater's forces had already shown their strength in creating GOP platform, Governor William Scranton refused to concede nomination till balloting began on convention's third day. Then his speech to delegates brought tears to eyes of his daughter Susan, 18.

7/16/64 — One campaign over, one battle won, Senator Barry Goldwater, the Republican nominee for President, bows head during benediction at close of convention, while his wife sheds tear of happiness. At left is former Vice President Richard Nixon, the party's standard-bearer in 1960 election.

7/16/64 — Republican presidential candidate Barry Goldwater poses with family. Seated on couch with the Senator and Mrs. Goldwater are daughters Joanne (left) and Peggy, and four grandchildren (Carolyn, Cynthia, Alison and Thomas). Immediately behind Goldwaters are sons Barry Jr., and Mike, who are flanked by Senator's sons-in-law, Dr. Thomas Ross and Richard Holt.

7/16/64 — Senator Goldwater's running mate, former GOP national committee chairman Congressman William E. Miller of New York, poses with his wife Stephanie (left) and daughters Elizabeth, 20, and Mary Karen, 17. Millers have two other younger children who did not accompany family to convention.

7/16/64 — A boy, a stream, a fishing pole and a sunny day all seem far removed from the field of political conventions and campaigns, but who knows what a lad dreams at such times. This serious-minded youth is Senator Barry Goldwater.

7/14/64 – Army chaplain presents flag from coffin of educator Lemuel Penn, a colonel in Army reserve, to his widow at burial services at Arlington National Cemetery. Penn was senselessly murdered by unknown assailants in Georgia.

7/16/64 – Freed by Federal Court order after serving some 10 years in prison for murder of his wife, Dr. Sam Sheppard kisses his German fiancee, Arienne Tebbenjohans, in Columbus, O. Court said Sheppard's trial had been mockery of justice.

7/18/64 – Ku Klux Klan burns cross at meeting in Irmo, S. C., during night meeting to hear address by Imperial Wizard Robert Shelton of Alabama. Spectators, including children, applauded lighting of the cross.

7/21/64 – Policeman struggles with woman demonstrator in Washington as hundreds of Cuban refugees attempted to storm Pan American Union Building where Latin American foreign ministers debated sanctions against Cuba.

7/23/64 – Representative of N.A.A.C.P. is forced to take refuge in his car after appealing to Negroes in Bedford-Stuyvesant section of Brooklyn to cease rioting. Violence came after series of riots in Harlem. Mayor Robert Wagner warned that "mob rule" would not be tolerated by the police.

7/20/64 — While waiting to greet visitors on White House lawn, President Lyndon Johnson showed that even heads of state run dry.

ROCHESTER, N.Y.

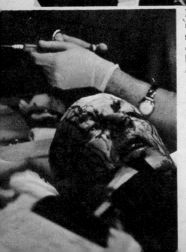

7/28/64 — When two Rochester, N. Y., policemen arrested a drunk, they were jumped by six Negroes; the scuffle that ensued touched off bitter racial riots, mass looting, which wasn't halted until Governor Nelson Rockefeller ordered 1,100 National Guardsmen into city. On second night of violence, State troopers force Negro into squad car (top photo), while morning after (middle photo) police patrols search Negroes on streets for weapons, evidence of looting. One of many casualties was police officer Louth Gaylon (left), his face streaked with blood upon entering hospital after suffering head and facial injuries.

7/26/64 — Teamsters President James Hoffa leaves Chicago courtroom after Federal jury found him guilty of fraud and conspiracy in connection with union funds. It was his second conviction.

7/28/64 — Mrs. Joan Kennedy, wife of Senator Edward Kennedy, smiles brightly after visiting him in Boston hospital to which he was recently transferred after suffering servere injuries in air crash.

7/31/64 — Two ages of man and sea cross off Brenton Reef near Newport, R. I., when Danish square rig trainer "Denmark" is over-taken by new nuclear-powered commercial vessel "Savannah." Both ships are visiting Providence.

7/29/64 — Astronauts Edward White (left) and James McDivitt, assigned to Gemini space program, display model of two-man spacecraft which will be used in the program. Hatches are designed to swing open, will be tried on orbital flight.

MOON SHOT

7/28/64 — Shortly before noon, Ranger 7 spacecraft thunders into skies above Cape Kennedy on first leg of 228,000-mile trip to moon. Fired by an Atlas-Agena rocket, Ranger 7 blasted off without a hitch; it's mission — to photograph surface of moon, relay pictures back to earth. Almost three days later, its six cameras began grinding some 1,300 miles from moon, kept sending photos till moment of impact. Picture below was taken at a distance of 480 miles and duplicates current Earth-based photography.

7/31/64 — Scientists at Jet Propulsion Lab in Pasadena, Cal., where moon probe was planned, rejoice at success. Ranger 7 scored "bullseye," transmitted pictures some 1,000 times better than taken by telescopes. Objects only three feet long could be identified.

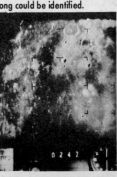

7/31/64 — President Lyndon Johnson holds first meeting with Joint Chiefs of Staff since General Earle Wheeler (second from left) was named chairman. Left to right, are Army Chief Gen. Harold Johnson, Wheeler, President Johnson, Air Force Gen. Curtis LeMay, Navy Adm. David McDonald and Marine Lt. Gen. W. M. Greene.

NATIONAL NEWS-END

INTERNATIONAL NEWS

7/2/64 — Princess Margaret, wearing low-cut, 18th century costume, complete with smoke-blue periwig, attends a benefit ball for London's St. John's Church.

7/2/64 – Soviet Premier Nikita Khrushchev and his wife Nina greet Norwegians who turned out to see them on visit to Oslo. Afterward he expressed pleasure at being able to meet people directly, something he was denied on visits to Denmark and Sweden where strict security measures were invoked.

7/6/64– Greek General George Grivas (left), hero of Greek-Cypriot battle for independence, shakes hands with U. N. representative Galo Plaza of Ecuador. Grivas pledged support for United Nations.

7/6/64 – Gustavo Diaz Ordaz is given Mexico City's version of ticker-tape parade after his election as nation's President. He succeeds Adolfo Lopez Mateos. Both are members of Institutional Revolutionary Party (P.R.I.) which hasn't lost a national election in 30 years.

7/9/64 – Rare photo of three daughters of Soviet Premier Nikita Khrushchev is snapped in Oslo, where they accompanied him on tour. Left to right, they are Mrs. Julia Gontar, 46 (daughter by his first wife), Jelena Khrushchev, a 26-year-old lawyer, and Rada Adzhubei, who is 34.

7/8/64 — World's only woman premier, Mrs. Sirima Bandaranaike of Ceylon, enjoys laugh with President Kwame Nkrumah of Ghana at opening of Commonwealth Premiers' Conference in London.

7/8/64 — Using artificial light native women plow field with primitive tools near Salisbury, Southern Rhodesia. Women claim they must work at night because authorities will not permit them to work by day. Nation's white minority (221,000) has allegedly limited political activity of the country's 3.9 miltion Africans.

7/8/64 — Moise Tshombe (left) announces to press conference he has successfully formed government of "new men" to administer the Congo. The new Premier, who returned from exile after having been ousted as President of Katanga province, was fourth to occupy post in nation's short, four-year history. His cabinet encompassed both left and right wing groups, but he saved four positions for himself (Foreign Trade, Planing, Information, and Foreign Affairs). Out-going Premier Cyrille Adoula (right, second photo) tried to force Tshombe to accept Mrs. Catherine Tshibamba (left) as Minister of Labor, but new Premier refused, eliminated post.

7/8/64 — Small girl sits upon rubble after earthquake caused widespread destruction in Coyuca De Catalan, Mexico. Thousands of scorpions crawled from torn earth to plague survivors.

195

7/11/64 — American student Paul Jasper cuts sugar cane on farm in Las Villas Province, Cuba. He put in two-hour stint in fields, along with others in 46-member student group traveling in interior of the island. Students made trip to Cuba in defiance of State Department edict.

7/15/64 — Cuban dock workers cheer in Havana as first shipment of 16 Leyland buses is lowered from East German freighter "Heinrich Heine." Vehicles are part of a purchase of 950 buses Cuba made from a firm in England. Ship also delivered cargo from Finland and East Germany.

7/15/64 — Soviet Premier Nikita Khrushchev listens attentively at joint session of Supreme Soviet in Moscow after naming Anastas Mikoyan (left) to post of President. Leonid Brezhnev (center) became Khrushchev's aide, possibly his heir.

7/17/64 — Women of Indian community in Msimbizi, United Republic of Tanganyika and Zanzibar, march in annual "Saba Saba" day procession, carrying sign professing loyalty to Mwalimu (translated: leader) Julius Nyerere, President of the newly-united nation in Africa.

7/21/64 — Cuban newspaper headlines charge made by Raul Castro, Cuban Minister of Armed Forces and brother of Premier Fidel, that U.S. Marines at Guantanamo Bay Naval Base shot and killed a Cuban sentry, whose picture is on page one. U.S. denied charge, saying Cuban sentries fired one shot at Marines, who then fired once into the air.

7/4/64 — Premier of Kenya, Jomo Kenyatta, relaxes at garden party at his house in Nairobi and picks a Kikuyu woman for partner in impromptu African "hoedown."

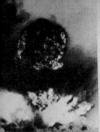

7/21/64 —World's largest, unconfined non-nuclear explosion bursts skyward in Alberta, Canada. One million tons of TNT was exploded in joint experiment by Canadian, British and American governments. Blast was the result of two years of planning.

7/24/64 — Body of Vietnamese officer is loaded into small boat in Vi Thanh, Viet Nam, after his infantry batallion was ambushed by Viet Cong troops. Forty were killed before relief came. One American sergeant was missing and believed captured while an American officer was wounded.

7/27/64 — Juana Castro Ruz, sister of Cuban Premier Fidel Castro, talks to newsmen in Mexico City. She announced she had fled Cuba, had requested political asylum from government of Mexico.

7/27/64 — While tourists from both North and South Korea look through windows, armistice talks between North Koreans and Communist Chinese (on left) and United Nations Military Command, led by U.S., begin their 12th year, the longest military armistice in recorded history. Talks drag on day after day in Panmunjom and consist of charges and counter charges. Table is set on truce line.

/28/64 — Sir Winston Churchill, 89, is presented with scroll by British Prime Minister Sir Alec Douglas-Home after making his farewell appearance in Parliament. He was first elected in 1900 as a Conservative, bolted party for Liberals, but 20 years later returned to Tories. Former Prime Minister Harold Macmillan said Churchill was "unique," that younger members would "never see the like again."

7/29/64 — Religious "prophetess" Alice Lenshina, whose fanatical followers believe she rose from the dead 11 years ago, was sought by 2,000 Northern Rhodesian soldiers after she declared "holy war" against government. Her followers staged bloody rebellion in which some 300 men, women and children were shot, hacked and burned to death. When her forces were cornered by government troops they refused to surrender, attacked boldly, believing Alice's boast that bullets used against them would turn to water. They didn't . . . 65 died.

7/26/64— On anniversary of his revolution, Cuban Premier Fidel Castro held press conference for foreign newsmen, including 25 Americans, in Santiago. He listens as official talks, later said he wanted direct negotiations with U.S.

7/29/64 — Rescue workers pour wine into small shaft bored down to trapped miners in Champagnole, France. Nine men were known to be alive after being trapped 7/27. Progress was slow, but steady, and officials hoped to rescue men within 24 hours.

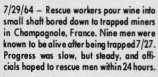

7/29/64 — Alexei Adzhubei, editor of Isvestia, and son-in-law of Russian Premier Nikita Khrushchev, pauses to chat with apprentice worker during visit to factory in Essen, West Germany. Interpreter is at right.

7/29/64 — While civil rights continued to create controversy across nation, pretty Dorothy Johnson, 18-year-old Negro coed from Idaho (second from left in last row), became first of her race to make finals of Miss USA contest in Miami Beach's Miss Universe Pageant. Other finalists were (front row, left to right) Toye Esch, 20, Oregon; Dorothea Langhans, 20, New York; and Jackie Maloney, 18, Oklahoma. In second row are Janet Erickson, 22, Utah; Pamela Borgfeldt, 20, Alabama; Johanna Reid, 18, Kentucky; Barbara Richartz, 19, New Jersey and Patricia Marlin, 21, Alaska. In last row are Gail Krielow, 20, Ohio; Miss Johnson; Diane Balloun, 19, Texas; Royette Tarry, 19, Maryland; eventual winner Bobbi Johnson, 19, District of Columbia; and Jeanne Venables, 23, California.

7/6/64 — Ron Musson, driving Miss Bardahl (U-40), leads Miss Exide, driven by Bill Brow, in Gold Cup race on Detroit River. Musson averaged 108.104 mph for three heats to win the event for unlimited hydroplanes.

7/22/64 — World champion racing driver Jim Clark slams into curve during Formula One Grand Prix in Stuttgart, Germany. He went on to win race, averaging 147.2 kilometers per hour.

7/30/64 — Miss Universe finalists pose before judging in Miami Beach. International pageant was won by Miss Kiriaki Tsopei of Greece (second row, middle). Other finalists are (front row, left to right) Miriam Brugada, Paraguay; Olga Monica del Carpio Oropeza, Bolivia; Edith Noel, France; and Lana Yi Yu, Republic of China. Second row are Emanuela Stramana, Italy; Bredna Blackler, England; Miss Tsopei; Angela Vasconcelos, Brazil; and Mercedes Revenga, Venezuela. In back row are Jorunn Nystedt, Norway; Siv Marta Aberg, Sweden; Ronit Rinat, Israel; Bobbi Johnson, United States; and Maria Amelia Ramirez of Argentina.

7/10/64 — American golfer Tony Lema lives up to nickname of Champagne Tony as he toasts his victory in the British Open at St. Andrews in Scotland. He battled high winds, top international field to win by five strokes. It was his fourth victory in six weeks.

7/16/64 — Cardigan Bay (7), top pacer from New Zealand and Australia, noses out American champion Overtrick (8) to win $25,000 Dan Patch Pace at New York's Yonkers Raceway. Winner set new track record for the mile of 1:58.2.

7/8/64 — On comeback trail, former heavyweight champion Floyd Patterson (right) jolts Eddie Machen in earning 12-round decision in Stockholm, Sweden.

7/31/64 — Walter Richardson of Minneapolis' Gopher Swim Club churns to new record of 57.5 seconds in winning men's 100-meter butterfly during U.S. Senior National AAU Outdoor Swimming Championships at Los Altos, Cal.

7/19/64 — Bobby Nichols, who had earned but $15,000 on professional golf tour all year, shows check for $18,000 to his wife for winning PGA championship at Columbus (Ohio) Country Club. He set 18-hole record of 64 in first round, and also set new PGA mark of 271 for 72 holes.

7/31/64 — Dick Roth of Santa Clara Swim Club receives victory kiss from sister Sandy after breaking world's record for 400-meter men's individual medley by full two seconds at AAU Championships in Los Altos, Calif. His time was 4:48.6.

7/8/64 — Skippers of five American 12-meter yachts shake hands before final trials off Newport, R.I., to select American Challenge Cup defender. They are (from left) William Cox, American Eagle; Charles Hovey, Easterner; Ted Hood, Nefertiti; Eric Ridder, Constellation; and Walter Podcak, Columbia.

/31/64 — A witch tossing away
er broomstick? Nope! Just a long-
aired English lass tossing javelin.

7/12/64 — The last-place Kansas City A's didn't have enough problems but what they had to chase horses. Steed was part of promotion stunt (nine were to be given away), but this one didn't take to idea, had to be run down by Jim Gentile.

7/16/64 — New switch on mail-order brides found Inga-Britt Granberg, 21, of Sweden (above) and Brian Cole, 33, (left), planning on wedding in six months. Brian, an Englishman, despaired of finding a bride at home, threw 1,232 bottles into the sea, each one containing a "lonely hearts" note. He received 381 replies, but Inga wasn't one of them. She read about his sea-borne pitch for romance in a magazine and wrote him a letter. He visited her in Sweden, now she will meet his parents in England.

7/27/64 — Designer Jacques Esterel fits scarf on model Bibelot in Paris. She needed it, since Jacques had given her a "new" look by shaving off all her hair.

7/11/64 — Los Angeles Dodger coach Leo Durocher, 58, poses with 26-year-old Carolyn Morin in Middlebury, Vt. Her father filed $150,000 alienation of affection suit against peppery baseball personality, claiming he was monopolizing attention of Carolyn's mother. Carolyn testified Leo proposed marriage to her and she turned him down; but hinted she might reconsider. Leo won case, too.

7/5/64 — Miss Jan Barthel, out for a day of sun at Lake Havasu, Ariz. City, attracted attention of Deputy Sheriff Terry Connell. Latter thought Jan was sporting new topless bathing suit (left), but found there were two sides to the question.

7/16/64 — Mrs. Henry Blaesing, 44, of Glendale, Calif., admitted in copyrighted story to "Los Angeles Herald-Examiner" that she was the "love child" of President Warren G. Harding and Miss Nan Britton, now of Chicago. Latter claimed she had affair with Harding from 1906 to 1922.

7/24/64 — Jack Van Deutekom, 25-year-old janitor (in window), holds knife to chest of his two-year-old son, screaming "I want to see my wife" in San Jose, Calif. At time his wife was in hospital giving birth to their second child. Police kicked in door to flat, subdued Van Deutekom.

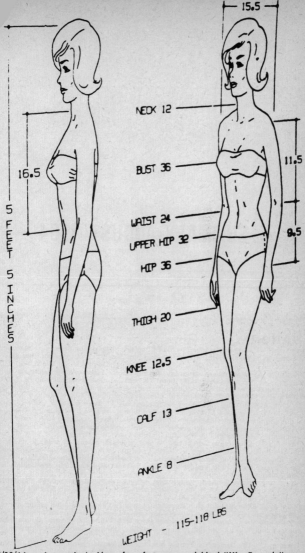

5 FEET 5 INCHES

16.5

15.5

NECK 12

BUST 36

WAIST 24

UPPER HIP 32

HIP 36

THIGH 20

KNEE 12.5

CALF 13

ANKLE 8

11.5

9.5

WEIGHT - 115-118 LBS

7/29/64 — Automation's idea of perfect woman, dubbed "Miss Formula" was turned out by electronic computer at California Computer Products, Inc., in Los Angeles. Engineers toiled for week, assembling data on what the perfectly formed woman should be, then fed results to computer. Latter cranked out measurements above (highly commendable by a layman's figuring), but obviously flunked drawing.

JULY – END

SUMMARY- AUGUST 1964

NATIONAL

Three bodies found by the FBI outside Philadelphia, Miss., were identified (August 4) as the civil rights workers missing since June 21 . . . Racial violence flared in Paterson and Jersey City, N.J., in Chicago and in Philadelphia . . . The A.F.L.-CIO Executive Council authorized a broad program for labor to help implement civil rights . . . Sheet Metal Workers Local 28, with an all-white membership of 3,300, voted to end nepotism and racial discrimination in accepting apprentices . . . Four men were arrested (August 7) in Georgia for the shotgun murder of Negro educator Lemuel A. Penn, a Lt. Colonel in the Army Reserve, on July 11. Penn was shot while driving back to Washington, D.C., after a refresher training course in Fort Benning, Georgia . . . A jury later (August 25) indicted three of the men for the murder. The fourth was reported to have turned states evidence . . . School integration below the college level was carried out peacefully in Mississippi.

Congress voted (August 8) to give President Johnson power to retaliate against hostile military action by North Viet Nam in any way he saw fit. The vote was unanimous in the House; in the Senate there were two dissenting votes . . . Congress passed and sent to President Johnson a Defense Bill authorizing expenditures of $46.7 billion.

Pierre Salinger, former Press Secretary to Presidents Kennedy and Johnson, was appointed to fill the Senate seat of Democratic Senator Clair Engle who died five months before his term expired.

President Johnson signed (August 20) an anti-poverty bill calling for expenditures of $947.5 million. The President named Peace Corps Director Sargent Shriver to head the campaign . . . The House voted 218-175 to bar Federal Courts from hearing complaints about the unconstitutionality of the apportionment of state legislatures.

The Democratic Party's National Convention opened in Atlantic City on August 23. President Johnson and Senator Hubert H. Humphrey of Minnesota were unanimously nominated for President and Vice President respectively on the first ballot . . . The Democratic platform named the John Birch Society in a condemnation of extremist groups.

The family fortune of President Johnson was revealed as amounting to $3.5 million.

Senator Barry M. Goldwater, Republican presidential nominee, rejected the support of the Ku Klux Klan. The Senator also rejected extremism at a Republican

Summit Meeting held at the Eisenhower farm in Gettysburg, Pa., and promised to seek advice from Eisenhower and Nixon on the appointment of a Secretary of State and a Secretary of Defense.

The **Federal Communications Commission** ruled (August 1) that as of November 1 idle chatter by ham radio operators would be barred . . . **In New York,** a man who had served a term of six years for assault by shooting was indicted for murder when the victim died ten years later.

The **Columbia Broadcasting System** bought control of the New York Yankee baseball club, paying $11.2 million for 80 per cent of the stock . . . **Hurricane Cleo** struck (August 26) the U. S. mainland from Key Largo to West Palm Beach . . . The **U. S. Census Bureau** officially named California (August 31) as the most populous state. New York had been number one.

The **unemployment rate** fell to 4.9 per cent (August 7), the first time in four years that the rate had fallen below five per cent.

The **first Catholic Mass** in English took place in St. Louis (August 24).

The **Paramount Theatre** in Times Square, N. Y., one of the country's best known movie palaces since 1926, to close, following the sale of the Paramount Building (August 4) . . . **Richard Burton's "Hamlet"** closed in New York after a record run of 136 performances. Previous record of 132 was established by John Gielgud in the theatre season of 1936-37 . . . **The marriage of stage star Ethel Merman** and movie and TV star Ernest Borgnine broke up in less than a week.

INTERNATIONAL

North Viet Nam torpedo boats fired on U. S. destroyers in international waters 30 miles off the North Vietnamese coast (August 2). The next day, President Johnson ordered the navy to destroy any future attackers. On August 4, further attacks brought retaliation by navy planes against the mainland. **Navy fliers** destroyed 25 boats and 90 per cent of the oil installations in the bases from which the hostile boats operated. **Premier Khrushchev** declared (August 8) that Russia would fight to defend North Viet Nam . . . **In South Viet Nam,** Major General Nguyen Khanh, head of the Military Revolutionary Council, deposed President Duong Van Minh and took over the office himself (August 16), **Rioting by students and Buddhists** forced Khanh (August 25) to resign the Presidency. For a few days the country was ruled by a military triumvirate, but on August 31 Khanh took over again, this time as premier . . . **An official of the Central Intelligence Agency** (CIA) expressing serious doubts that victory can be won in Viet Nam suggested (August 22) a negotiated settlement.

Leftist rebels opposed to the rule of Premier Tshombe in the Congo captured Stanleyville, chief city of north Congo.

Turkish planes raided the Greek areas of Cyprus causing considerable damage and many casualties (August 8). The next day the U.N. Security Council by a vote of 9-0, with Russia and Czechoslovakia abstaining, called for an immediate cease-fire. Both Turkey and Greece accepted the demand. Greece and Turkey returned to the North Atlantic Treaty Organization armed forces from which they had withdrawn to assure world peace.

The **first encyclical** issued by Pope Paul VI (August 10) offered his services to assure world peace.

Palmiro Togliatti, head of the Italian Communist Party, largest of the free world, died at the age of 71 (August 21) and was succeeded by his chief deputy, Luigi Longo.

Brazil devalued the cruzeiro (August 13) by almost 10 per cent . . . **Bolivia** broke relations with Cuba (August 21).

SPORTS

Australian swimmer Murray Rose broke the world's record for 1500 meters with a time of 17.01:8 against the previous record of 17.05:5 (August 2).

Ludvik Darick, a 27-year-old Czech, established a new world mark for the discus throw, 211 ft. 9 in. Old mark was 206.6 (August 2).

Northern Dancer, winner of the 1964 Derby and Preakness, was injured and reported unlikely to race again.

For the first time since 1954, the U. S. won both national tennis doubles titles. Chuck McKinley and Dennis Ralston captured the men's crown for the third time in a row and Billie Jean Moffitt teamed with Mrs. Karen Hanze Susman to take the women's doubles.

OBITUARIES

Ian Fleming, 56, creator of the James Bond character in novels about the British Secret Service, on August 13.

Gracie Allen, partner (and wife) of George Burns in vaudeville, radio and TV, on August 27 at the age of 58.

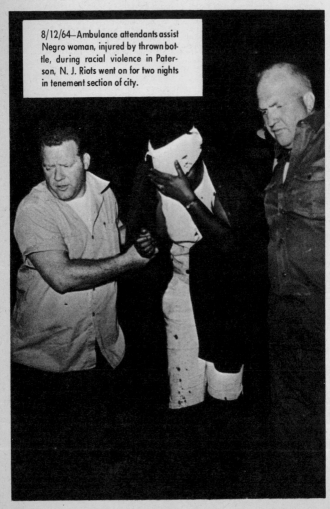

8/12/64—Ambulance attendants assist Negro woman, injured by thrown bottle, during racial violence in Paterson, N. J. Riots went on for two nights in tenement section of city.

NATIONAL NEWS

8/3/64 — Police Sergeant James Simpkins carries badly wounded Louis Mitchell from riot-torn housing center in Jersey City, N. J., on second night of racial violence in the city. Negroes objected to arrest of a Negro woman for drunkenness, went on three-day rampage.

8/3/64 — With pistols drawn, police challenge Negro occupants of car in Jersey City, N. J., on second night of racial violence. Night before 32 persons, including 17 policemen, were injured in riots.

8/4/64 — Negro clergymen cruised Jersey City streets in car equipped with loudspeaker in effort to halt racial riots. Negroes hurled stones, Molotov cocktails at police. Mayor Thomas Whelan took firm stand against rioters, called it "a simple case of hoodlumism." More than 65 were arrested in three nights. Similar outbreaks of racial violence occurred in Elizabeth and Paterson, N. J.

MISSISSIPPI

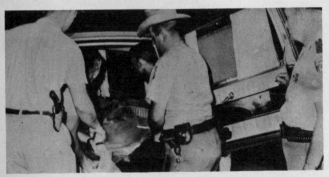

8/5/64—Authorities remove one of three bodies of civil rights workers from ambulance at University of Mississippi Medical Center in Jackson, Miss. The bodies of Michael Schwerner, 24, and Andrew Goodman, 20, both white, and Negro James Chaney, 24, were discovered by FBI agents buried 25 feet down in an earthen dam near Philadelphia, Miss. They had been missing since June 21, one day after arriving in Mississippi to assist in civil rights-inspired voter registration drive. Two days later their burned station wagon was discovered, but widespread search failed to locate bodies. Both Schwerner and Goodman had been shot through the heart, while Chaney was beaten severely. FBI refused to comment on how bodies were discovered, but $25,000 reward had been offered. Negro comedian Dick Gregory was active in case.

8/7/64—Robert Goodman comforts wife on arrival of son's body at Newark Airport.

8/7/64—Family of slain civil rights worker, James Chaney, are emotionally overcome following the brief funeral service in Meridian, Mississippi.

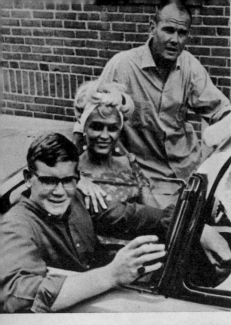

8/6/64 — Sam Sheppard Jr. (left) is reunited with his father (right) when latter was released from prison, having served 10 years after being convicted for murder of his wife. In center is Sheppard's bride, German-born Arianne Tebbenjohanns Sheppard, who worked for his release. Photo was taken in Cleveland.

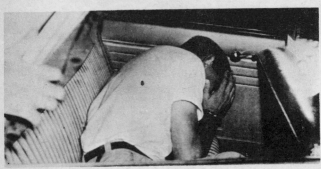

8/6/64 — James Lackey, 29, hides face in Atlanta, Ga., after confessing to taking part in shotgun slaying of Negro educator Lemuel Penn last month. He implicated three other men, all Ku Klux Klan members.

8/9/64 — Black Muslim leader Elijah Muhammad addresses 5,000 followers in Los Angeles, as heavyweight champion Cassius Clay (right) listens attentively. Muhammad told crowd that U.S. Negroes will separate themselves from white community completely by the end of this decade.

8/6/64 — U.S. sailor and his girl say last good-bye before his ship, guided missile frigate, "Coontz," left for the Far East.

8/8/64—Luci Baines Johnson, 17-year-old daughter of President Johnson, dances the "Watusi" with actor Steve McQueen at a celebrity-studded "LBJ" barbecue sponsored by "Young Citizens for Johnson" in Beverly Hills. Luci and her sister Lynda have agreed to make five public appearances to aid her father's election campaign.

8/10/64—President Lyndon Johnson signs Congressional resolution backing his "fight-if-we-must" stand on Southeast Asia, prompted by incident in Gulf of Tonkin where North Viet Nam torpedo boats attacked U. S. ships. Congressional leaders look on.

8/13/64 — Restaurant owner Lester Maddox (dark suit) autographs axe handle for patron at his Atlanta, Ga., restaurant. Axe handles were used by Maddox last month to drive Negroes from his restaurant, which he refuses to integrate. He sold axe handles as souvenirs, later defied court order to desegregate. Next day, bottom photo, he wept as he announced to crowd that he was closing his restaurant "forever" rather than admit Negroes.

8/12/64 – Uniformed and plainclothes policemen use night sticks to disperse rioters in Elizabeth, N. J. Hundreds of Negro and white youths roamed dock area in packs, hurling fire bombs and rocks at cars, smashing windows. Two policemen in patrol car were attacked by youths.

8/14/64 – Police Captain Lloyd Sealy (right) inspects squad before it goes on duty in Harlem. Sealy was put in command of Harlem precinct, the first of his race to hold post.

8/18/64 – Upside down? Well, the picture isn't, but astronauts Ted Freeman (left) and Edwin Aldrin are as they perform weightlessness tests in special aircraft.

8/21/64 – Dr. Aaron Henry (left), chairman of Mississippi Freedom Party, arrives in Atlantic City, N. J., for Democratic Party Convention. He seeks to have his delegation seated in place of all-white Mississippi group.

8/24/64 – Dr. Martin Luther King addresses CORE demonstrators on boardwalk at Atlantic City. Group is protesting seating of all-white delegation from Mississippi at Democratic Party convention.

8/24/64 – Members of George Lincoln Rockwell's American Nazi Party are searched by police in Atlantic City after they became involved in tussle on boardwalk. Fight started when someone threw a punch at one of the Nazis.

8/25/64 – Attorney General Robert Kennedy, flanked by New York's Mayor Robert Wagner and Mrs. Kennedy, formally announces he is a candidate for Democratic nomination for U. S. Senator from New York.

8/25/64 – Three sons of the late President Franklin D. Roosevelt meet at Democratic Party Convention in Atlantic City. Left to right they are James, Elliot and Franklin Jr. Fourth son, John, is a Republican.

/64 – Republican presidential
ndidate Senator Barry Goldwater holds informal press conference aboard his pleasure craft
"Sundance" off Catalina Island.
Senator was vacationing before
beginning his campaign.

8/27/64 – President Lyndon Johnson and Sen. Hubert Humphrey of
Minnesota, the President's personal choice for Democratic vice presidential nomination, wave to convention delegates after Humphrey's acceptance speech in Atlantic City. Second photo at right
shows Senator's wife Muriel with
her two young grandchildren, Jill
and Vicki Solomonson, at the Humphrey's home in Waverly, Minn.

8/27/64 – Before leaving for convention and his acceptance
speech, President Johnson took
helicopter to Winchester, Va.,
where he attended funeral services for wife of Senator Harry F.
Byrd. In an emotional moment,
President kissed Senator's hand.

8/27/64 — Hurricane Cleo, with winds up 100 miles an hour, ripped through Mia Beach, leaving trail of broken windows, fallen trees. Photo at left is of damage at Hotel Doral. Despite severity of winds, no deaths resulted.

8/29/64 — Angry Negro woman shakes fist at helmeted policeman, who keeps gun hand ready, as mass looting, rioting goes on in Philadelphia, Pa. Shortly after photo was taken, photographer Frank Johnston of U.P.I. was injured. More than 150, including 35 policemen, were wounded in two days; 165 were arrested.

NATIONAL NEWS-END

THE CONGO

8/4/64 — Premier Moise Tshombe receives warm welcome from tribesmen in Kivu Province (top photo) on tour to unite feuding tribes in the Congo. Despite enthusiasm of natives, Tshombe's troubles were not lessened as rebel troops led by pro-Communist Gaston Soumaliot continued to threaten his rule. Later in month Tshombe used white mercenaries, who combined with Congolese Army to drive rebels from Bukavu (bottom photo). Bitter fighting left many dead in streets.

8/27/64 — Crowd of children and adults run to greet Congolese government troops which arrived to reinforce liberating forces that drove pro-Communist rebels from Bukavu. In other African nations, crowds protested use of mercenaries.

VIET NAM

8/5/64 — North Viet Nam PT boats, of Soviet P-4 Class (top photo), attacked U. S. destroyers in Gulf of Tonkin, touching off crisis in Southeast Asia. President Johnson ordered counterattack at North Viet Nam PT bases. Some 25 boats were destroyed. At same time, Defense Secretary Robert McNamara ordered "substantial military reinforcements," including F102 Delta Dagger Jets (middle photo) to Saigon. Despite attacks, U.S. destroyer "Maddox" (bottom photo) continued to cruise in area in support of aircraft carrier "USS Ticonderoga."

8/31/64 — In addition to war with Communist-led Viet Cong, South Viet Nam was thrown into internal strife as Buddhists and Catholics waged undeclared but bloody war against each other. Both fear other will gain control of government and persecute the loser. Top photo shows Buddhist youths after they attacked, burned Catholic village of North Viet Nam refugees. Picture of late President Ngo Dinh Diem, a Catholic, was found in a house. Catholic mobs protested in Saigon, denouncing Buddhist "neutralist" stand against Communists. Catholic youths at right, armed themselves, one with a hand saw, the other with machete and a makeshift shield.

8/17/64 — Northern Rhodesian policeman leads two bewildered children to safety after they wandered from Chiboma village during fighting between government forces and fanatical religious followers of "prophetess" Alice Lenshina. Insert shows injured woman with child by her side during fighting. Scores were killed before Alice was captured, called off "Holy War." Charges against her were dropped.

8/7/64 — Five Cuban refugees arrive at immigration headquarters in Ft. Lauderdale, Fla., after being picked up off Grand Bahama Island. They fled Cuba in improvised raft of rubber inner tubes lashed together with bamboo.

8/5/64 — Nine miners, rescued from cave-in near Champagnole, France, pose on hospital balcony where they are recuperating after being trapped nine days. Rescue efforts continued for five still trapped.

CYPRUS

8/9/64— Cypriot PT burns off Xeros after being attacked by Turkish Air Force jets. Turkey ordered air strike to relieve pressure on besieged Turk-Cypriots.

8/16/64 — Indian Commander of U.N. Peace-Keeping Force on Cyprus, Gen. Thimayya, mops brow during press conference. Earlier, he had stated cease-fire between Turkish and Greek Cypriots was "only a breather." He later toned down statements, presumably after rebuke by U.N. Secretary General U. Thant. Latter's special representative on island, Senor Galo Plaza of Ecudaor, relaxed after negotiating with Greek-Cypriots.

8/5/64 — Mrs. Ruth Habwe speaks to group of women near Nairobi, Kenya. She is running for seat in national legislature and campaigning for equal rights for women. In this regard, she is urging tactics of Aristophanes' "Lysistrata" (411 B.C.), a Greek comedy in which the women refused to sleep with their husbands until they stopped waging war. Eight men are opposing Mrs. Habwe.

8/10/64 — Royal holiday finds Princess Anne and her father Prince Philip (with cap on) lounging on the royal yawl "Bloodhound" off Cowes, Isle of Wight, England. Princess Anne was 14 four days after photo was taken.

8/17/64 — Moderator Edler Garnett Hawkins, first Negro to head United Presbyterian Church of U.S.A., meets with Pope Paul VI, at latter's summer residence at Castelgandolfo, Italy. Two men at right are unidentified.

8/22/64 — Crowds swarm around coffin of late Italian Communist Party leader Palmiro Togliatti as it arrives in Rome. The 71-year-old party leader died after suffering a stroke while on vacation in Soviet Union.

8/20/64 — American-born Queen Hope of Sikkim arrives in New York with six-month-old son Prince Palden on visit to World's Fair. The 22-year-old Queen is former N.Y. debutante.

8/24/64 — Dr. Manuel Antonio de Varona y Loredo dictates letter to his wife Olivia, who serves as his secretary in offices of Cuban Rescue Committee in New York. Dr. de Varona, 55, is former Premier of Cuba, and now heads anti-Castro group, while supporting himself as car salesman.

8/24/64 — Soviet newspaper "Izvestia" published this photo in Moscow, showing American aircraft "buzzing" Russian motorship "Georgia," while latter was underway. Photo was offered as proof of remarks made by Soviet Premier Nikita Khrushchev that Russian ships had been "buzzed" by U.S. planes on 1,000 occasions.

INTERNATIONAL NEWS-END

8/20/64 — Bronze statue, created by sculptress Harriet Frishmuth and borrowed from Metropolitan Museum of Art, is displayed at World's Fair (opposite page).

←————————————

8/13/64 — Actress Elaine Stritch turned down summer theater tours and spent off-season serving as a barmaid in New York (right). Here she talks with patrons while serving up three long beers.

8/1/64 — Marilyn Ramenofsky, 17, of Scottsdale, Ariz., churns to new world's record in women's 400-meter freestyle in finals of AAU swimming championships at Los Altos, Calif. Miss Ramenofsky was clocked in 4:42.8, some 2.8 seconds faster than old mark. Total of nine world and 20 American marks were broken in meet.

8/13/64 — New York Yankee slugger Mickey Mantle hammers second homer of day against Chicago White Sox. Earlier, while batting left-handed, Mickey slammed 500-foot-plus homer (see arrow), the longest ever recorded in Yankee Stadium. Blow went over screen, in centerfield, landed in 15th row of the bleachers.

8/12/64 — Rebecca Welles, 19-year-old daughter of actress Rita Hayworth and Orson Welles, is kissed by Michael Flores, 21, to whom she will be wed. Both are studying at Pasadena (Cal.) Playhouse.

8/5/64 — Geraldine Chaplin, 19-year-old daughter of world famous comedian Charlie Chaplin, on vacation at San Lorenzo, Italy.

8/13/64 — World heavyweight champ Cassius Clay and his new bride, Chicago model Sonji Roi, 24, in L. A.

8/20/64—Greek sprinter Evangelos Marcellus takes Olympic torch from Aleca Katselli on first leg of flame's trip to Japan.

8/24/64—Frank Capsouras, 17, leaps for joy after setting American teen record in Olympic weight-lifting trials.

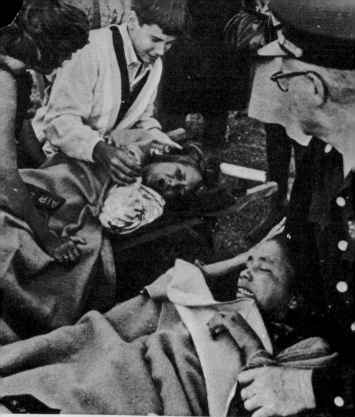

8/18/64—Disaster? Well, not quite. It's just hysterical teen-agers being comforted by friends after being overcome with emotion in San Francisco at sight of their heroes. Who are the heroes? Who else? The Beatles from Britain!

8/2/64—Miss Kiriaki Tsopei takes a playful kick at sands of Miami Beach morning after she won Miss Universe contest. She was representative of Greece.

8/23/64—Veteran driver Bill Horstmeyer, 35, is killed as his car leaps off northwest turn (background), skims fence and flips over three times during running of Tony Bettenhausen Memorial 100-Mile Auto Race at Illinois State Fair.

8/30/64—New distance-running sensation Bob Schul crosses finish line at Woodland Hills, Cal., setting world record of 8:26.4 for the two miles.

8/3/64—Mickey Mantle, Jr., 11-year-old son of Yankee slugger, lines up putt. Boy can drive a golf ball 200 yards.

**ENTERTAINMENT
SPORTS & THE ARTS
END**

MISCELLANY

8/11/64—Attorney Newton Schwartz accompanies clients wearing party masks to conceal identity on way to Federal grand jury gambling investigation in Houston, Tex.

8/6/64 — James Alfano, 24, full-time policeman and sometime skydiver, rests in Chicago hospital after surviving 7,000-foot fall. He bailed out, fell 5,000 feet in free fall, then pulled his ripcord. Parachute failed to open, so he pulled emergency chute. Latter became entangled with main chute and he hit ground with neither fully opened. He walked away.

8/15/64—Plainclothes detective pins two unruly girl demonstrators against a tree in New York City. Girls were part of protest march before United Nations. They were demonstrating against United States action in South Viet Nam.

8/11/64—Sand-covered car, with body of 33-year-old Elizabeth Jones in trunk, is unearthed at Lake City, Fla. Her ex-husband, Odell, 31, said he pushed her into pool where she drowned, then put body in trunk and dug all day to bury car.

8/16/64—Mrs. Marie Miller, 23-year-old Ohio divorcee with two children, may join harem of Sheik Suleman al Huzail of Beersheba, Israel. Sheik has had 53 wives but never more than four at one time. He has offered $50,000 to the American woman who will spend one year in his harem. She will take children with her.

AUGUST – END

SUMMARY - SEPTEMBER 1964

NATIONAL

The AFL-CIO endorsed President Lyndon B. Johnson for re-election in November (Sept. 1).....**Robert F. Kennedy** was nominated by New York Democrats to run for the U.S. Senate against incumbent Republican Senator Kenneth Keating..... **Barry M. Goldwater,** opening his campaign (Sept. 3) in Prescott, Arizona, called for an end of the draft..... Robert F. Kennedy resigned (Sept. 3) as Attorney General of the U.S...... **Strom Thurmond,** Democratic Senator from South Carolina resigned from the Party to become a Republican.... **Hearst newspaper** group announced support for President Johnson in the election, first Democrat endorsed by the papers since the first administration of Franklin D. Roosevelt..... Governor George Romney of Michigan, appearing on the same platform as Senator Barry Goldwater in Detroit, refused to accept the latter's endorsement of support in his campaign for re-election as Governor..... **Scripps Howard** newspapers support Johnson.

A New York grand jury absolved Police Lieutenant Thomas R. Gilligan of criminal responsibility in the shooting of a 15-year-old Negro boy which triggered the July riots in Harlem and Brooklyn..... **Teen-age rioting** marked Labor Day across the country..... **Two white men** were acquitted (Sept. 4) of the murder of Washington, D.C., Negro school superintendent Lemuel Penn in Georgia in July. **Mr. Penn,** a Lt. Colonel in the reserves, was shotgunned to death while driving home from an army refresher course in Fort Benning..... **A boycott of New York City schools,** staged by white parents in protest against the busing of children to schools outside their immediate neighborhoods in order to establish a racial balance, was partially successful (Sept. 14) when 275,638 children stayed out of school, 27% of total enrollment. However, school authorities pointed out that normal daily absenteeism amounts to around 100,000. On the second day of the boycott, 22% of the enrollment were absent..... **Three Federal judges in Birmingham, Alabama,** ruled the Civil Rights Law unconstitutional in the application of its public accomodations provisions to certain restaurants.....

The Anti-Defamation League reported (Sept. 19) that many top corporations and wealthy individuals contribute to extreme right wing organizations..... A poll of New York City whites revealed that a majority thought the Negro drive for civil rights had gone too far..... **The FBI** released a report stating that the epidemic of rioting which swept the country during the summer was not basically a racial protest but anti-authority in character.

President Johnson announced the development of a system for destroying satellites (Sept. 17)..... **A new poison** which kills only rats was demonstrated in New York..... Utility companies announced a new device which permits the reading of meters by telephone.

Chrysler Corporation and United Auto Workers union signed (Sept. 9) a three-year contract calling for the largest pensions — up to $400 — in the history of labor..... Ford Motor Company signed (Sept. 18) a similar contract..... Negotiations between General Motors and the union broke down and the union called a nation-wide strike against the company on September 25..... **Federal minimum wage** was raised from $1.00 to $1.15 per hour, increasing the pay of an estimated 565,000 workers (Sept. 3)..... N.Y. longshoremen's strike tied up ports from Maine to Texas.

The U.S. Senate voted (Sept. 10) 75-3 to reopen the investigation into the affairs of Robert G. Baker, former Secretary to the Democratic Senate Majority..... **The Judiciary Committee** of the U.S. House of Representatives by a vote of 20-13 ordered (Sept. 22) an investigation of the Justice Department for the possible violation of the constitutional rights of individuals..... **The U.S. Senate** voted (Sept. 24) a resolution stating that it was the "sense of Congress" that Federal Courts should move slowly in ordering the reapportionment of state legislatures under a recent Supreme Court ruling..... On the same day, **three Federal judges cancelled the November elections** for the Connecticut state legislature because of the failure of the state assembly to provide for reapportionment in a recent special session.

The Florida coast was hit by Hurricane Dora (Sept. 9) and the Carolinas suffered extensive damage from Hurricane Gladys on September 18 ..... A prolonged drought, called the worst in history, resulted in forest fires in New Jersey, the closing of parks in Westchester County, New York.

A group of parents in the high-income suburb of Darien, Connecticut, were arrested (Sept. 21) for serving liquor to minors at private parties after a 17-year-old girl was killed in an auto accident following one of the parties ..... Six ticket-holders won $100,000 each in the New Hampshire State Lottery, first legalized lottery in the nation's history..... **Vonda Kay Van Dyke** of Arizona won the Miss America title..... **Edward M. Gilbert,** absconding promoter, pleaded guilty (Sept. 25) to stealing $2 million from a publicly-owned company he headed..... New York City's population passed the eight million mark, making the city third largest in the world after Tokyo and London.

The commission headed up by Chief Justice of the United States Earl Warren released its report on the assassination of President John F. Kennedy, affirming that Lee Harvey Oswald was solely responsible for the crime.

Secretary of State Dean Rusk announced (Sept. 29) that Red China would soon explode a nuclear device.

INTERNATIONAL

Gen. Nguyen Khanh was reinstated (Sept. 3) as Premier of South Viet Nam. On Sept. 8 Maj. Gen. Duong Van Minh was named chairman of a triumvirate of generals to rule the country ..... An attempted military coup against Premier Khanh collapsed (Sept. 13)..... In Tokyo (Sept. 28) Assistant Secretary of State William McGeorge Bundy said that communist pressure could force the expansion of the war outside of S. Viet Nam.

The Soviet Union said that Red China was claiming 500,000 square miles of territory belonging to the Soviet Union and other nations (Sept. 1)..... A posthumously revealed letter of Italian Communist leader Togliatti criticized the Soviet Union for splitting the communist world..... Britain and the Soviet Union signed the largest commercial contract ever when Britain sold the Soviets (Sept. 7) an $84 million synthetic fiber plant and granted a 15-year credit for 80 per cent of the purchase price..... Leftist rebels in the Congo set up an independent government of a "Peoples Republic of the Congo"..... Uruguay broke off diplomatic and commercial relations with Castro Cuba (Sept. 8)..... An agreement between the **Hungarian government and the Vatican** restored Catholic rights in Hungary after a lapse of 20 years ..... Wills Stoph succeeded Otto Grotewohl as Premier of East Germany..... Senator Eduardo Frei was easily elected President of Chile over a communist-backed candidate.

The Third Session of the Ecumenical Council Vatican II, originally summoned by the late Pope John XXIII to review Catholic credos in the modern world, opened in Rome (Sept. 14)..... On Sept. 29, by a vote of two to one, the Council approved membership in the order of deacons for married men of mature age. This was the first exception to the rule of celibacy for the priesthood in 900 years.

Bolivia crushed (Sept. 20) a right wing attempted coup..... General de Gaulle, President of France, departed for Venezuela to begin a tour of 10 Latin American countries — the longest trip abroad ever undertaken by a French ruler.

The island of Malta became an independent state after 35 centuries of foreign domination.

SPORTS

Roy Saari, 19, swam the 1500 meters in 16.58:7 in the U.S. Olympic Trials to become the first man ever to swim the distance in under 17 minutes ..... **Rex Cauley**, a 24-year-old graduate student at the University of Southern California, broke the old world's record of 49.2 seconds for the 400-meter hurdle with a mark of 49.1 ..... **Terje Pederson**, 20, of Norway became the first man ever to throw the javelin more than 300 feet when he set a new world mark of 300 feet 11 1/2 inches.

Roy Emerson of Australia won the U.S. men's tennis title at Forest Hills. **Maria Bueno** of Brazil took the women's title.

The yacht "Constellation" maintained the unbroken U.S. supremacy in the America's Cup races by defeating the British challenger, "Sovereign," in four straight.

OBITUARIES

Sergeant Alvin C. York, 76, America's most famous winner of the Congressional Medal of Honor in World War I (Sept. 2).

Sean O'Casey, famous playwright, in England at the age of 84 (Sept. 18).

Otto Grotewohl, 70, Premier of East Germany.

Гостиница „МЕТРОПОЛЬ"

г. Москва

I Lee Harvey Oswald do hereby request that my present citizenship in the United States of America, be revoked.

I have entered the Soviet Union for the express purpose of applying for citizenship in the Soviet Union, through the means of naturalization.

My request for citizenship is now pending before the Supreme Soviet of the U.S.S.R.

I take these steps for political reasons.

My request for the revoking of my American citizenship is made only after the longest and most serious considerations.

I affirm that my allegiance is to the Union of Soviet Socialist Republics.

[signature]

COMMISSION EXHIBIT No. 913

NATIONAL NEWS

9/27/64—Almost 10 months to day it was appointed, seven-member Warren Commission, appointed by President Lyndon Johnson to investigate assassination of John F. Kennedy, submitted 706-page report in Washington, D. C. Commission heard testimony from 552 witnesses, assembled hundreds of exhibits on every facet of case, including letter above by Lee Harvey Oswald asking revocation of his U. S. citizenship. Commission concluded he was assassin, acting alone.

9/27/64—Above is Commission exhibit #1303, a 6.5mm model 91/38 Mannlicher-Carcano rifle, owned by Oswald, which was shown to be weapon which killed the President. Oswald bought it from mail-order house, using name of A. Hidell. Opposite page shows three photographs of Oswald; two at left were taken during his stay in Russia, where he met his wife. Photo at right shows him in 1963.

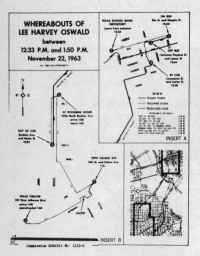

9/27/64—Warren Commission assembled maps showing Oswald's movements from 12:33 p.m. to 1:50 p.m. on day of assassination, Nov. 22, 1963. Commission members actually paced many of the distances involved to determine if Oswald could have covered territory specified in time allotted. After leaving assassination scene, Oswald was apprehended by policeman J. D. Tippit. Twelve persons witnessed shooting of Tippit, and seven positively identified Oswald as the killer.

9/27/64—Commission reenacted assassination, using Oswald's rifle with camera attached to telescopic sight. With aid of films taken at scene, by amateur photographers, Commission was able to pinpoint spot where President was hit. Camera revealed Oswald had clear line of fire. F.B.I. showed rifle was capable of hitting moving target from such a distance.

PHOTOGRAPHS OF LEE HARVEY
➤ OSWALD TAKEN IN MINSK

COMMISSION EXHIBIT 2891

COMMISSION EXHIBIT 2892

PHOTOGRAPH OF LEE HARVEY OSWALD ◀
PROBABLY TAKEN IN LATE SEPTEMBER, 1963

(COMMISSION EXHIBIT 2788)

9/1/64—Rev. John Cross stands at pulpit of Sixteenth Street Baptist Church in Birmingham, Ala., after repair work was completed, following bomb blast last year which took lives of four young girls.

9/16/64—Shaykh M. Hassen and Raymond Hall (left) in police headquarters in Philadelphia after being arraigned on charges of inciting racial riots in North Philadelphia. Florence Mobley at right, voluntarily surrendered. Police raided Black Nationalist headquarters, confiscated guns, steel clubs, Molotov cocktails.

9/1/64—Helmeted police officer holds suspected looter with one hand, and recovered goods in the other on second day of racial riots in Philadelphia. More than 150 were injured, 165 arrested on first day of disorder. Violence at first seemed senseless, but police eventually uncovered cause (see above).

9/1/64—For first time, Negro students attend previously all-white schools in Greenville, S. C. Negroes went virtually unnoticed as city peacefully integrated its public schools.

9/2/64—Dr. James S. Murphy and his wife, the former Victoria Thompson (left, above), arrive to testify at State Supreme Court hearing in White Plains, N.Y., over custody of his four children by his first wife, Mrs. Nelson A. Rockefeller (right, above). She relinquished custody when she obtained divorce.

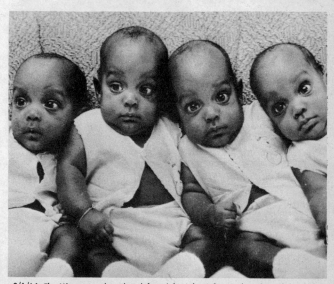

9/1/64—The Mincey quadruplets, left to right, John, Luke, Mark and Matthew, pose for formal portrait in Cincinnati. At three and one-half months of age, they are so similar parents need identification bracelets to tell them apart.

243

9/3/64 — Workmen prepare the "Aluminaut", a unique submarine, for launching in Groton, Conn. The 50-foot sub is designed to dive to depth of three miles. It was built by General Dynamics.

9/3/64 — Lon Dunaway, 28, a member of the American Nazi Party, is led away by police in Washington, D. C., after he attacked a witness before House Un-American Activities subcommittee. Witness was denouncing investigation of travel to Communist countries as a "farce." Dunaway jumped on table, tried to throttle the witness.

9/5/64 — Carolyn King (center), escorted by two members of her family, is heckled by white youths as she walks to school in Birmingham, Ala. She had previously registered at all-white Jones Valley High School.

9/6/64 — Father Leo Rosconiec, a Spanish-speaking priest, talks with group of migrant Puerto Rican farm workers in Edmore, Mich., after they were stranded there when pickle plant they were working in closed. Workers threatened to burn plant, but were calmed by priest and local officials, who promised them aid.

9/8/64 — Robert F. Kennedy, Democratic candidate for U. S. Senate from New York, is mobbed by admirers in Buffalo. Enthusiastic crowds frequently forced his motorcade to come to a halt.

STUDENTS RIOT

9/7/64—Labor Day weekend saw outbreak of student rioting on both coasts. At Seaside, Ore., (top right), 2,000 teen-agers kept police hopping for two nights, while in Hampton Beach, N.H. (right), State National Guardsmen were called out to quell more than 10,000 disorderly youths. More than 165 were arrested in New Hampshire.

9/8/64—Under the shadow of Coogan's Bluff in New York, where baseball history from John McGraw to the Mets was made, the Polo Grounds is destroyed to make way for housing project.

9/3/64—Luci Baines Johnson, 16-year-old daughter of President Lyndon Johnson, shakes off Washington protocol with an enthusiastic version of the "frug" at a fashion show in Capital's Mayflower Hotel. Her partner here is Joe Piro, a professional dancer, who is known as Killer Joe.

9/10/64—Hurricane Dora slammed into Florida's eastern coast, bringing two days of torrential rains, abnormal tides and winds up to 125 miles-per-hour. Above, winds whip palms in St. Augustine as two youths slosh along bayfront street. Below, woman and children view damage to their home in Jacksonville Beach while, on opposite page, President Johnson examines storm damage. Only three died in storm, but damage ran to $200 million.

HURRICANE DORA

9/14/64 — Negro boycott at elementary school in Cleveland, O., found only 13 of 40 pupils present in second grade classroom. School is where young minister died in civil rights demonstration when he tried to halt construction by throwing himself under bulldozer.

9/11/64 – L.B.J. made trip to Jacksonville, Fla., to inspect hurricane "Dora" damage.

9/14/64—Massive police patrols were assigned to guard grade school in Jackson, Miss., on first day of integration. Nine Negro students were enrolled in first grade. No incidents occurred to block desegregation.

9/16/64—Rev. K. L. Buford (left) and Dr. Stanley Hugh Smith, a professor, after their precedent shattering election to city council in Tuskegee, Ala. They defeated white opponents in a run-off election.

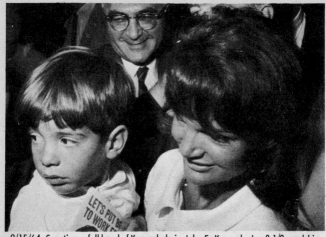

9/15/64—Sporting a full head of Kennedy hair, John F. Kennedy Jr., 3-1/2, and his mother Jacqueline visit campaign headquarters of his Uncle Bob in New York.

9/15/64—Teacher directs students at New York City school after arrival by bus as first of group in new plan by school officials to end racial imbalance in school system. Plan called for busing students from predominantly white schools into areas where students are mainly Negro and Puerto Rican and vice versa. White parents protested plan, staged boycott on opening day.

9/21/64—Mr. and Mrs. Charles Cutler admire new roof on their house which is situated on land owned by Mrs. Lyndon B. Johnson, the President's wife, in Autagaville, Ala. Their home, and others, were recently in national spotlight when Republicans "investigated" conditions of Mrs. Johnson's tenants after President had proposed a program to eliminate poverty.

9/21/64—The U.S.S. Atlanta, a World War II cruiser, was selected by Navy to be test ship in first simulated nuclear air blast test on a manned combat ship. Ship will be subjected to battering of shock waves from 500-ton TNT explosion in Hawaii, while crew will be "buttoned up" below decks. Ship was given $4 million conversion for series of three blasts which will test new metal alloys.

9/23/64—The controversial XB70A jet bomber, which was to have been the B70 but was later relegated to experimental status, lands at Edwards Air Force Base in California after maiden flight (top photo). Flight was not without incident. Fire broke out and, on landing, two tires blew out (directly above) on giant bomber, which is designed to fly at better than 2,000-miles-per-hour. Over $1.5 billion has been spent on development of the giant super-sonic jet.

9/23/64—Fire fighters cover their faces with water-soaked burlap bags to protect them from intense heat of flames from forest fire in Agua Caliente, California. High winds sent fire raging through Kentwood area of town, threatened other communities. More than 30,000 acres were scorched by runaway blaze.

9/25/64—Mexican President Adolfo Lopez Mateos and U. S. President Lyndon B. Johnson, and their wives, embrace in middle of International Bridge in El Paso, Texas. They met there to celebrate agreement ending century-old territorial dispute caused by shifting in course of the Rio Grande River.

9/23/64—Lloyd Shaw, one of four men trapped in Atomic Energy Commission test hole in Nevada desert, is helped into waiting ambulance. They were trapped four days when cable snapped, killing one man on surface. What with overtime, etc., pay for each could top $1,000.

9/28/64—Firemen attach chain to twisted wreckage of Burlington Railroad engine after it crashed with Rock Island passenger train in Montgomery, Ill. They pulled one crewman alive from wreckage but he died later. Three others died, 48 were injured in crash.

9/28/64—Soldier fires Army-Marine Corps new "Redeye" guided missile at China Lake, Calif. New lightweight weapon is designed for use by foot soldiers. It weighs 28 pounds, fires much like a bazooka, but has no "kick." First test was success.

9/28/64 — Julie Nixon, 16, (L) and her sister Tricia, 18, daughters of former Vice President Nixon, accepted honorary chairmanships of Youth for Goldwater and Miller. Girls were photographed in New York State campaign headquarters.

9/29/64—President Johnson visits Senator Edward Kennedy in Boston hospital where he is recovering from injuries received in air crash. Senator's wife Joan looks on. Photo was first taken of Sen. Kennedy when he was not strapped to Stryker frame (in background) which was used to speed his recovery.

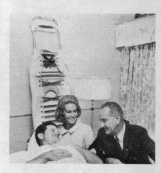

9/30/64—The YF-12A takes off from Edwards Air Force Base in California on first flight. All-weather intercepter can do 2,000 mph, reach 70,000 feet.

9/4/64—Standing hip-deep in wheat is Soviet Premier Nikita Khrushchev on tour of farmlands in Kazakhstan in Southeastern Russia.

, 1/64—Roman Catholic rioters dare Buddhists to retrieve
a dying comrade following
attack on Catholic high school
in Saigon, Viet Nam. In all,
three died as rival religious
groups clashed.

/5/64 — Congo Premier
Moise Tshombe is carried in
triumph into Albertville, after
his troops liberated city, following three months of occu-
pation by rebel forces.

/14/64—Attendants and fellow Cardinals rush to aid of
James Francis Cardinal McIntyre after 78-year-old Archbishop of Los Angeles
collapsed during opening
ceremonies of Ecumenical
Council in Rome. His condition was listed by an aide as
"not grave."

/14/64 — The Toonerville
trolley? Not by a long-shot!
It's a mobile atomic power
station built by the Soviet Union. Powered by uranium, the
caterpillar-tractor unit can
supply electricity wherever it
goes. It will develop 1,500
kilowatts and will work for
one year without reloading.

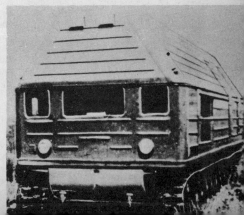

9/11/64 — Socialist-Communist party members pay off on election bets in Santiago, Chile, dunk themselves in fountain after defeat.

9/14/64—Angolan National Liberation Army men check map before launching attack against Portuguese Army positions in Angola. Nationalists have been active for two years in effort to win for African nation independence from Portugal.

9/11/64—Lt. General Aly Amer confers with other military men in Alexandria, Egypt, during Arab Summit Conference meeting. He is Commander of Joint Arab Defense Forces, says Egypt alone could defeat Israel in a war.

9/14/64—Premier Nguyen Khanh (center) and Viet Nam Chief of State Duong Van Minh (left), are all smiles after having put down an attempted coup in Saigon. Army generals sought to overthrow Khanh's government, but were repulsed without bloodshed.

9/18/64—With crowns held high, King Constantine, 24, of Greece takes a queen in Athens by marrying Princess Anne Marie of Denmark. More than 6,000 Greeks were invited to wedding reception. U. S. was represented by Miss Lynda Bird Johnson.

9/19/64—Pope Paul VI receives Rev. Martin Luther King and Rev. Ralph Abernathy, American civil rights leaders, in audience in Vatican City. King said Pope promised statement on race relations.

9/14/64—Members of Britain's Royal Ulster Rifles assist women and children from truck which brought them from Indonesian Borneo to Sarawak. Refugees claimed that they had been victims of ill-treatment from Indonesian troops.

9/22/64—Labor Party leader Harold Wilson (left) lights up pipe while former Prime Minister Earl Attlee puffs on his during strategy conference in London. Lord Attlee led Labor Party in four general elections, while Wilson will be at head of party for first time in general elections next month.

9/23/64—Pope Paul VI bears bust of St. Andrew at Ecumenical Council in Rome. Priceless relic was sent to Greek Orthodox Church as unity gesture.

9/24/64—Workmen widen opening in Berlin Wall after West and East German governments agreed to permit West Berliners to visit relatives in East.

9/24/64 — Widow of Mexican bandido Pancho Villa tells newsmen in Chicago her husband stole "a little" but gave money to poor.

9/25/64—Marie Louise Monnet, a leader of Catholic Woman's group, arrives at Vatican City. She is first woman permitted to attend Ecumenical Council.

9/29/64--Throng of youngsters trails after blindfolded Indonesian paratrooper, being led by tommy-gun wielding British Gurkha in Labis, Malaysia. Indonesian soldier was captured in dense jungle area some 100 miles from Singapore.

9/28/64--Archbishop of Canterbury, Dr. Michael Ramsey (right), greets 89-year-old Patriarch of Moscow and All Russia, His Beatitude Alexii, in London. Latter's visit, his first to England, returns Dr. Ramsey's '62 trip to Russia.

ENTERTAINMENT
SPORTS & THE ARTS

9/2/64—Roy Saari, 19-year-old USC swimmer, is congratulated by his father after shattering 17-minute barrier for 1,500-meter swim. Saari set new world record for metric mile of 16:58.7 at Olympic Trials in New York

9/1/64—Masonori Murakami, 20-year-old lefthanded pitcher for San Francisco Giants, signs autographs for fans in New York City where he joined team for series against the Mets. Murakami, who had impressive record in minor leagues, is first Japanese player er to make the major leagues. A relief specialist, Murakami made debut by pitching one scoreless inning

9/3/64—Fourteen-year-old Leonore Modell of Sacramento, Calif., gets kiss from her coach, Paul Herron, after she became youngest swimmer ever to cross the English Channel. She made trip from Cape Gris Nez, France to Dover, England in 15 hours, 32 minutes.

4/64—Israeli actress Dahlia Lavi is center of attention of beach in Venice where she attended film festival.

9/8/64—Britain's Beatles seek refuge in paddy wagon to avoid throngs of fans after tumultuous performance in Toronto.

9/10/64—Band-leader Xavier Cugat, 63, announces engagement to Charo Baeza, 18-year-old Spanish singer with his band.

9/11/64—Daisy Voog, 26, after becoming first woman to climb Mt. Eiger in Alps.

9/9/64—Miss Universe, Kiriaki Tsopei of Greece (right), and Bobbi Johnson, Miss U.S.A., pose in Tokyo garden while on a good-will tour to Japan.

9/11/64—Robert Froner, 22, and his bride of four months show off winning ticket after he hit record "twin double" payoff of $172,726.80 in N.Y.

9/12/64—Vonda Kay Van Dyke, 22-year-old Miss Arizona, manages weepy smile after winning Miss Congeniality trophy in Miss America pageant at Atlantic City, N.J. Later in evening, the 5-6, brown-haired beauty won top prize, Miss America.

9/15/64—Heavyweight champion Cassius Clay and his wife arrive in New York where he will train for title fight on Nov. 16 in Boston against ex-champ, Sonny Liston.

9/16/64—Michael Glennon, 21, of Los Angeles, poses in cockpit of low-slung dragster racing car after arriving in Southhampton, England, for competition there. His car can do better than 200 miles-per-hour from a standing start over a quarter-mile track, needs a parachute to stop.

9/15/64—Sister act? No! At left is photo of late movie queen, Jean Harlow, while at right is actress Carroll Baker, who will play Miss Harlow in new film.

9/9/64—Juan Garcia Mondeno (center, above) takes his place in procession of Dominican monks in Caleruega, Spain. One of that nation's top matadors (see right), he shocked bullfighting world by giving up career in bullring to join religious order.

9/21/64—New York football Giant's championship hopes came tumbling down in Pittsburgh when Steeler lineman John Baker charged into quarterback Y. A. Tittle (top left). Tittle was sidelined for second half; Giants suffered second loss.

9/22/64—Dejected crew member of British yacht Sovereign after losing final race to Constellation, successful defender of America's Cup, off Newport, R. I.

9/22/64—Joe Louis Barrow Jr., son of former heavy-weight boxing champ, chats with classmate as he begins freshman year at Boston U. Joe Jr. plans to study law.

9/29/64 — America's Chuck McKinley tosses racquet aside after losing to Australia's Roy Emerson in Cleveland. Match enabled Aussies to recapture Davis Cup.

9/22/64—Wrapped in terrycloth poncho, Soraya, Ex-Queen of Iran waits for the cameras to roll in Sardinia, Italy where she is making her debut in movies. Scene is on yacht and is one of three episodes from the film which is entitled "Three Faces Of A Woman."

9/23/64—American soprano Leontyne Price (left) receives tremendous ovation at Bolshoi Theatre in Moscow after she appeared with La Scala Opera Company in performance of Verdi's "Requiem." Conductor Herbert Von Karajan receives flowers for Miss Price. Ovation lasted 26 minutes.

9/20/64—Billy Campbell of Huntington, W. Va., holds trophies after winning U. S. Amateur Golf Championship in Cleveland. He beat Ed Tutwiler of Indianapolis in close match, one-up over 36 holes.

9/4/64—Willie Heiligh is bathed in cement after newly-poured concrete floor fell on him, four others in Washington.

9/25/64—With head held high, temperamental turtle gives the back of his foot to a buddy who has eye on his dry perch in a lake in St. Petersburg, Florida.

9/28/64 — Ten-year-old Mike Grost hits the books after signing up as full-time student at Michigan State U. A whiz at math, Mike had been taking courses at school for over a year before becoming its youngest regular student.

9/29/64—Leicester Hemingway, younger brother of the late novelist Ernest Hemingway, points map showing "Republic of New Atlantis," an island he built on rock shelf in 50 feet of water off Jamaica. Wife Doris and daughters look on. As honorary president, he plans to issue stamps, meanwhile continuing work of raising the Republic from the sea.

9/26/64—Kids are pretty much the same in Savannah, as elsewhere. Or are they?

SEPTEMBER – END

SUMMARY - OCTOBER 1964

NATIONAL

A federal court issued an injunction (Oct. 1) against a strike of long-shoremen which had tied up shipping from Maine to Texas. The United Auto Workers ended (Oct. 25) their month-long strike against General Motors.

The Federal Communications Commission (FCC) ruled that the Republican Party was entitled to equal time to compensate for broadcast news conferences held by President Lyndon B. Johnson.... For the first time in its 124-year history, the New York Herald-Tribune supported a Democrat for the Presidency by backing President Johnson against Senator Barry Goldwater.... Life Magazine announced its support of Johnson, the first time it had backed a Democrat for President since it was founded in 1936.... Goldwater forces accused Governor Nelson Rockefeller of New York of willfully withholding support in the presidential campaign.... A House subcommittee cleared President Johnson and other government officials of any wrong-doing in the case of Billie Sol Estes.... Walter W. Jenkins, special assistant to President Johnson, resigned (Oct. 14) after revelation of his arrest in Washington, D.C., on a disorderly charge.

The Sheriff of Neshoba County, Miss., his deputy and three other men were arrested by the FBI on charges of having violated Negro civil rights (Oct. 3)....
Malcolm X, former Black Muslim leader, announced (Oct. 3) that he no longer held his former racist beliefs.... New York City parents staged a school sit-in (Oct. 6) to protest busing of children to schools outside their own neighborhoods in a plan to establish racial balance. Sixty-five parents were arrested.... Dr. Martin Luther King, Negro civil rights leader, was awarded (Oct. 14) the Nobel Peace Prize for 1964.

The Congress gave President Johnson a victory in refusing to support a Congressional curb of the U.S. Supreme Court's order to the states to reapportion their legislatures on a population basis.... The 88th Congress adjourned (Oct. 3) its final session.

L. Judson Morehouse, former Chairman of the N.Y. State Republican Committee, was charged by a state assistant district attorney with having asked the Playboy Club to pay him $100,000 for helping them secure a liquor license.... Former Democratic Governor of Massachusetts, Foster Furcolo, was indicted (Oct. 13) with four of his former assistants on a charge of having conspired to obtain a bribe for members of his Executive Council.... Mafia leader Joseph (Joe Bananas) Bonnano was abducted in front of an apartment house on New York's Park Avenue hours before he was due to testify before a Federal Grand Jury.... Gems worth $380,000 including the world's largest star sapphire were stolen (Oct. 30) from the American Museum of Natural History in New York.... The 69-year-old Chief Justice of the

Louisiana Supreme Court got into a fist fight with a 66-year-old Associate Justice in the court chamber. The latter claimed that his colleague had called him an SOB.

A **New York court** ruled against Mrs. Nelson Rockefeller in her suit to obtain custody of her four children by her first husband. . . . **New York State's Appellate Division**, the state's second highest court, reversed a lower court's decision terming Mexican divorces illegal. . . . **The U.S. Supreme Court** agreed to review the government's curb on travel to Cuba. . . . A group of **prominent Catholic laymen** from several countries asked Pope Paul VI to review Catholic teachings on birth control.

Hurricane Hilda struck (Oct. 3) Louisiana near New Orleans causing $30 million of damage.

The New York World's Fair ended (Oct. 18) its first season with a profit of $12 million, considerably less than had been estimated.

INTERNATIONAL

In the largest mass escape since the Berlin Wall was erected in 1961, 23 men, 31 women and three children crawled to freedom through a tunnel under the wall (Oct. 3).

Queen Elizabeth and Prince Philip of England, ignoring assassination threats, were cheered and jeered on a visit to Canada.

President Nasser of the United Arab Republic held Premier Moise Tshombe of the Congo captive in Cairo as a hostage for the safety of Arab and Algerian embassy personnel in the Congo who had been threatened by the Congolese military. Tshombe had gone to Cairo as an uninvited guest at a conference of unaligned nations.

The deputy chief of the U.S. Air Mission in Venezuela was kidnapped by leftist terrorists and held as a hostage for a N. Viet Nam terrorist who was under sentence of death in S. Viet Nam. Authorities rescued him, arrested two of the terrorists (Oct. 9-12).

White mercenaries in the Congo mutinied against their German commander.

The Russians launched the first multi-manned vessel into space (Oct. 12) with a crew consisting of a cosmonaut, an engineer and a physician. . . . **French Communists** asserted their independence and called for non-interference in national affairs by outside Communist parties. . . . **Nikita Khrushchev was replaced as Premier of the Soviet Union** and boss of the Communist Party. K's protege, 57-year-old **Leonid Brezhnev** took over the Party job; Deputy-Premier **Aleksei N. Kosygin**, 60, moved up to become Premier. . . . **France** agreed to extend $350 million credit to Russia over a period of seven years. . . . **Red China exploded a nuclear device.** . . . **de Gaulle** backed the call of Red China's Premier Chou En-lai for a disarmament conference of the five member nations of the nuclear club—U.S., Gt. Britain, Russia, France and China.

The Labor Party of Gt. Britain won the national elections by a majority of four over the Conservative and Liberal parties. Labor chief Harold Wilson became the new Prime Minister (Oct. 15).

In a move interpreted as **support for Castro Cuba**, Spain called for non-intervention in the affairs of Latin-American nations (Oct. 12).

Pope Paul VI announced (Oct. 18) that he would fly to India in December for the World Eucharistic Congress in Bombay . . . . **Premier Ikeda** of Japan resigned because of illness . . . . Tran Van Huong was named new Premier of S. Viet Nam.

French author Jean-Paul Sartre rejected the 1964 Nobel Prize for Literature.

SPORTS

The New York Yankees won the American League pennant and the St. Louis Cardinals finished first in the National League. The Cards took the World Series, four games to three. Immediately following the Series, Yogi Berra was fired as manager of the Yankees and Johnny Keane, who had resigned as manager of the Cards, took over the Yankee job.

In automobile racing, **Graham Hill won the U.S. Grand Prix** at Watkins Glen for the for the third year in a row.

Art Arfons, a mechanic, set a new world's land speed record of 434.02 miles per hour, breaking the record of 413.20 m.p.h. set two days earlier by Tom Green. A week later (Oct. 13) Craig Breedlove lifted the record to 468.72 m.p.h., raised it to 526 m.p.h. on October 15 and then crashed.

The United States won the most gold medals in the Olympic Games in Tokyo, Japan. The U.S.A. team received 36 top awards to 30 for the Soviet Union. (Complete results page 289).

OBITUARIES

Cole Porter, one of the greatest song writers of all time, aged 72 (Oct. 15).

10/15/64 — America's Bob Hayes, after winning 100-meter semi-final in wind-aided 9.9 seconds. Later he won final in 10.0.

10/16/64 — Rev. Dr. Martin Luther King Jr., and his wife Coretta embrace happily in Atlanta, Ga., after learning that Dr. King was awarded Nobel Peace Prize for 1964. At 34, Dr. King is the youngest person ever so honored. He is also the 12th American, some of the others being Theodore Roosevelt (1906), Woodrow Wilson (1919), Dr. Ralph Bunche (1950) and Gen. George C. Marshall (1953). Nobel Prize Committee, as is its custom, gave no reason for the award, but did mention that Dr. King "follows the principle of nonviolence" as America's foremost Negro leader. He will donate entire award ($54,000) to civil rights movement.

NATIONAL NEWS

10/29/64 – Prof. Charles H. [...] receives call of congratulations [...] winning one half of 1964 Nobel Pri[...] for physics. Two Russian physicis[...] shared award with Townes who de[...]veloped "lasers" which led to revo[...]ution in radio and physics. He no[...] holds post of provost at MIT.

10/1/64 – In letter home, U.S. Nav[...] enlisted man, James Kress, of D[...]buque, La., told of "incident" in Gu[...] of Tonkin, two weeks before, an[...] named destroyers involved as h[...] ship, the R.S. Edwards, and the Mo[...]ton. Pentagon had acknowledged e[...] counter with North Viet Nam PT-boa[...] but didn't identify ships until lette[...] was published.

10/1/64 – U.S. Navy released th[...] photo of the top-side rudder of n[...]clear-powered submarine Threshe[...] which was lost with 129 aboard 22[...] miles off Cape Cod 18 months befor[...] diving bathyscaph Trieste II , ind[...]cated that the Thresher had broke[...] up, presumably from pressure, whi[...] making practice dive at depth of 8,40[...] feet.

10/5/64 – North American Aircraf[...] huge XB70 supersonic plane dwar[...] T-38 chase plane and helicopter [...] its second test flight at Edwards A[...] Force Base, Calif. Plane is designe[...] for speeds of up to 2,000 mph, b[...] no attempt was made to reach th[...] mark on one-hour flight.

10/6/64 – Rebuilt Presidential limo[...]sine, the same one in which Preside[...] Kennedy was assassinated, is used f[...] first time by President Johnson [...] Washington. Car's bubble-top was r[...]moved and is now permanently e[...]closed with bullet-proof glass, arm[...] plate. Hand grips on rear are f[...] Secret Service agents.

10/2/64 — Ripping its way through town of La Rose, La., a tornado signaled advance of Hurricane Hilda across state's bayou country. Tornado gouged mile-long path through town, killed 21, injured 160. Hilda came later with winds up to 130 mph, forcing marshlands residents to flee.

JOHNSON CAMPAIGN TOUR

10/11/64 — President Lyndon Johnson does some friendly finger shaking in Nevada.

10/6/64 — Speaking from rear platform of the "Lady Bird Special," Mrs. Lyndon B. Johnson addresses crowd in Richmond, Va., at start of her eight-state swing through Southern states on behalf of the President's bid for re-election. Daughter Lynda Bird also spoke to crowd, addressing her remarks to young voters. Later in month, President addressed 30,000 persons in Dayton, Ohio. Though crowd stretched as "far as the eye could see" it was far from the largest one he drew during campaign. Some 250,000 turned out to hear him in Louisville, Ky., 200,000 more in Des Moines, Iowa.

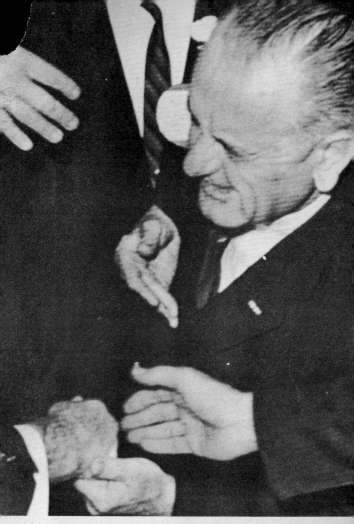

10/8/64 — Disregarding personal safety and displaying an old campaigner's love for crowds, President Lyndon Johnson engaged in extensive handshaking wherever he spoke, and at no small cost. Above, in Cleveland, he winced in pain and slipped forward after receiving strong handclasp on his bruised and bandaged right hand. In less painful moments, he addressed supporters warmly and, at times, fatherly, stressing peace and prosperity, and invoking image of the "Great Society," in which, he told audience in Pittsburgh, "nobody in this country is (going to be) poor." With all leading public opinion polls showing him far ahead, he asked nation to give him history's "greatest landslide."

275

10/12/64 — Republican Presidential candidate Sen. Barry Goldwater drew tongue twitching response from bespectacled calf at livestock show in Portland, Oregon.

GOLDWATER CAMPAIGN TOUR

10/24/64 — Chin strap on Mexican sombrero gave Sen. Goldwater some difficulty and a good laugh in San Diego, while wife Peggy received key to city on visit to her home town, Muncie, Ind. Despite polls predicting his defeat, Senator's campaign seemed to grow stronger as election neared. Crowds reacted enthusiastically to his charges that Democratic administration was "soft on Communism;" roared with delight when he referred to opposition's policies as "Daddyism." He pushed hard on issue of corruption, referred repeatedly to "curious crew" surrounding his opponent.

10/9/64 — Parents, whose children were affected by New York City's school busing-integration plan, begin 24-hour vigil in protest outside Mayor Wagner's home.

10/13/64 — Resident of Kingston, N.C., hauls his boat and trailer up State highway 55 which, like the rest of the town, was flooded by the Neuse River. Hundreds of families left town as river hit crest of 23 feet, nine above the flood stage.

10/15/64 — Air Force unveiled its revolutionary, variablewing, supersonic fighter, the F111, at General Dynamics plant in Fort Worth. Formerly known as the TFX, and the subject of a Defense Department contract controversy, the F111's most distinguishing feature is its wings, which can be swept back (top photo) to achieve speeds up to 1,600 mph, and can also be extended (bottom photo) for low-speed landings on short or unimproved runways.

10/14/64 — At height of election campaign, Democratic Party received jolt when it was revealed that Walter Jenkins, Special Assistant to President Johnson and a top aide of his for 30 years, had been arrested on a morals charge, his second in five years. Republicans demanded investigation of security aspects of case, while President requested and received resignation of Jenkins, who was hospitalized, suffering from "nervous exhaustion."

10/18/64 — Unisphere at twilight as New York World's Fair closes till Spring.

10/17/64 — Harvard biochemist Dr. Konrad E. Bloch (right) after winning half of Nobel Prize in Medicine and Physiology for work on cholesterol.

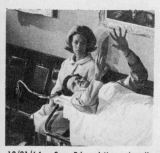

10/21/64 — Sen. Edward Kennedy tells newsmen in Boston hospital of plane crash in which he broke back last June. Wife Joan sits beside the Senator.

10/15/64 — Former Vice President Richard Nixon uses powder puff before facing television cameras, audience of 2,000 at Goldwater rally in Cleveland.

10/20/64 – Officers of multilateral crew of U.S. missile destroyer, "Claude V. Ricketts," confer as ship arrives in Washington. Seven nationalities are represented in crew. Four at left are officers from England, Italy, United States and West Germany.

10/22/64 – President and Mrs. Lyndon B. Johnson, followed at right by Senator Barry Goldwater, attend memorial services for former President Herbert Hoover in New York. A distinguished mining engineer and world-famed humanitarian prior to his election in 1928, Mr. Hoover was 90 years old when death came.

10/22/64 – Ellis Island, 27-1/2-acre island in New York Harbor, which has been gateway to U.S. for European immigrants for years, but is now closed, was subject of recommendation by Secretary of Interior that it be converted to national historical site.

10/22/64 – Astronaut John Glenn and wife Annie at their home in Texas where he said he would become director of Royal Crown Cola company. He is almost fully recovered from ear injury which cancelled political career.

10/26/64 – Carol Harrison, who dances in San Francisco under name of Exotica, holds photo taken of her in topless bathing suit. Picture was used, without her permission, in Republican campaign film. Movie was withdrawn from TV, but she wants to be paid any way; threatens suit.

DISTRICT OF COLUMBIA

OFFICIAL BALLOT

PRESIDENTIAL ELECTION NOVEMBER 3, 1964

Place a mark in the box beside the names of the
candidates for whom you wish to vote.

SAMPLE

Republican

☐ BARRY GOLDWATER, President, and
WILLIAM E. MILLER, Vice-President

Democratic

☐ LYNDON B. JOHNSON, President, and
HUBERT H. HUMPHREY, Vice-President

Fold Here
before leaving voting booth.

10/26/64 — Dancers do the "frug" at "political night club" in New York where entry fee is a "contribution" to Johnson campaign fund.

10/27/64 — Negro baseball star Curt Flood and wife enter home rented in Calif. Renting agent threatened to bar them.

10/27/64 — Copy of ballot Washington, D.C., residents will use to vote for President, the first time they've done so.

INTERNATIONAL NEWS

CARACAS - SAIGON

10/9/64 — U.S. Air Force Lt. Col. Michael Smolen, 45 (pictured with his family above), was kidnapped in Caracas, Venezuela, by Castroites in weird plot to obtain release of a Communist terrorist scheduled for execution thousands of miles away in Saigon. (See next page for results of international episode.)

10/19/64 — U.S. Embassy in Saigon won brief reprieve for Communist terrorist Nguyen Van Troi (at left) when Castroites kidnapped American officer in Venezuela. When American was eventually released unharmed, South Viet Nam government went ahead with execution of Troi, 17. He had been convicted of trying to assassinate Defense Secretary Robert McNamara in Saigon by planting a bomb under bridge over which McNamara was scheduled to pass.

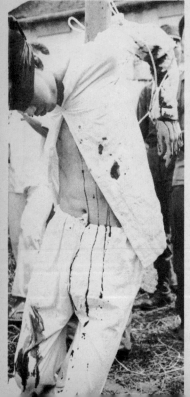

10/19/64 — Proclaiming his innocence, and shouting "Long live Viet Nam," Troi was tied to post, executed by firing squad. His limp body was then cut down, placed in plain wicker casket.

10/2/64 — South Viet Nam's three ruling generals (left to right) Premier Nguyen Khanh, Duong Van Minh and Tran Thein Kheim salute troops in Saigon before Kheim, who is opposed by Buddhists, left on extended foreign tour.

10/4/64 — Two Congolese children peer from behind fence at white Rhodesian mercenary in Lisala. Soldier was part of patrol moving against rebel forces which have been murdering hundreds of native civilians in embattled area of the Congo.

10/5/64 — U.S. Naval Base at Yokosuka, Japan, was scene of demonstration by some 15,000 students and union members in protest against negotiations between Japan and U.S. to berth nuclear submarines (without nuclear weapons) at the base.

10/8/64 — Heads of state (without their heads) wait before start of Cairo conference. Robes are Cyprus' Archbishop Makarios; interlocking hands, Ethiopia's Haile Selassie; hands in lap, Indonesia's President Sukarno.

10/13/64 — Soviet citizens present flowers to three hatless heroes in Moscow after trio returned from space following first multi-manned orbital flight. From left, they are Dr. K. Feoktistov, scientist Boris Egorov and Col. Vladimir Komarov who commanded the Voshkod space vehicle. None of the three wore space suits during flight.

BERLIN TUNNEL TO FREEDOM

10/5/64 — Six months of back-breaking and, at times, near-suffocating labor by 30 volunteers, starting from French sector of West Berlin, produced largest mass escape of refugees from East Berlin since wall went up in 1961. Workers dug 448-foot tunnel 35 feet under wall to East Berlin, enabling 57 to flee before Communists discovered tunnel. On opposite page refugees wait at West Berlin side before crude chair lift (above) will hoist them up to ground level and freedom.

KHRUSHCHE REPLACED

10/16/64 — After brief period of rumors, Russian news agency Tass announced that Nikita Khrushchev had been "released" from all duties, for reasons of age and health; was replaced by Leonid Brezhnev (left), Aleksei Kosygin.

10/23/64 — Khrushchev's ouster shocked both Western and Communist nations. After initial announcement, Pravda elaborated on reasons for his dismissal—errors of policy (presumably on China), nepotism and fostering a cult of personality. New Soviet heirarchy gathered (above) at funeral of Russian general. Kosygin (second from left) took over as Premier; while Brezhnev (fourth from left) held key post as head of party. Khrushchev's whereabouts were unknown but unconfirmed reports said he would occupy North Moscow apartment in building below.

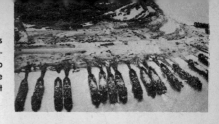

10/20/64 — On this day, 20 years ago, Gen. Douglas MacArthur returned, as he said he would, to The Philippines. Ships on Leyte beach were part of huge assault force.

10/16/64 — Labor Party leader Harold Wilson and wife wave to voters in Liverpool after he cast vote in national election. Next day he was Prime Minister after winning narrow victory, first for his party in England in 12 years. Laborites gained majority of only four seats (of 630) in Parliament.

10/15/64 — Bitterly denouncing her brother, Juana Castro holds press conference in Miami, her first stop on anti-Communist campaign throughout the hemisphere. She recently fled Cuba, said it and "the Americas" must be saved.

10/9/64 — Covering their faces against tear-gas fumes, women stage economic protest in Guayaquil. Ecuador. They carried national flag, sang anthem.

10/17/64 – Part of 5,000-man police force turned out to maintain order during Peronist rally in Buenos Aires, Argentina, fire tear gas bombs to halt march through city streets. Demonstrators were trying to arouse public sentiment in favor of ousted dictator Juan Peron.

10/23/64 – Newsmap pinpoints site of Communist China's first nuclear explosion, making her the fifth nation (U.S., Russia, England, France) with atomic weapons. Described as a "low yield" explosion, perhaps slightly less powerful than America's first (equal to 20,000 tons of TNT), it still prompted anti-bomb protests around the world. China lacks, however, bomb delivery system.

10/24/64 – Despite rain, Pope Paul VI stands in open car, extends hand to woman who reached out to him in Montecassino, Italy. Pope was leaving rebuilt Abbey of Montecassino (background) after consecrating it. Abbey was destroyed in World War II by Allies after Germans established observation post there.

10/27/64 – South Vietnam new Chief of State Phan Khac Suu (left) talks with Gen. Nguyen Khanh after latter resigned as Premier, post he had held in caretaker status for two months. Suu, elected by the High National Council, holds mainly ceremonial post, but will name next Premier.

10/22/64 — Kenya's Gov. Gen. Malcolm MacDonald dances with that nation's "First Lady," Mrs. Ngina Kenyatta, wife of Prime Minister, at Nairobi reception.

SOVIET UNION		UKRAINE		POLAND	
OWES	MARGIN	OWES	MARGIN	OWES	MARGIN
$52,623,137	$5,793,331	$6,777,577	$583,295	$3,665,051	$265,126
CZECHOSLOVAKIA		HUNGARY		BYELORUSSIA	
OWES	MARGIN	OWES	MARGIN	OWES	MARGIN
$3,537,004	$92,741	$2,095,699	$423,202	$1,773,220	$145,756
ROMANIA		YEMEN		PARAGUAY	
OWES	MARGIN	OWES	MARGIN	OWES	MARGIN
$1,268,194	$274,586	$141,467	$54,086	$132,490	$45,109

10/27/64 — Soviet Union and other nations risk losing votes United Nations General Assemb for non-payment of assessment Chart at left shows nations i volved and amounts each owe Margin amounts are sums eac must pay to retain vote.

10/28/64 — Indian student rea posters in New Delhi protestir forthcoming visit of Pope Paul to India. Religious groups dema Pope's visit be cancelled and th Christian missionaries leave cou try. Pope is to attend Eucharis Congress at Bombay next mont

10/28/64 — Five recently appoir ed Hungarian Catholic bisho (wearing kerchiefs around head are consecrated at ceremony St. Stephen's Basilica in Budapes Recent agreement between Va can and Hungarian governme permitted appointment of the fi religious leaders.

INTERNATIONAL NEWS-END

BASKETBALL
Team—United States

BOXING
Flyweight—Fernando Atzori, Italy.
Bantamweight—Takao Sakurai, Japan.
Featherweight—Stanislav Stepashkin, Soviet Union.
Lightweight—Jozef Grudzien, Poland.
Light Welterweight—Jerry Kulej, Poland.
Welterweight—Marian Kasprzyk, Poland.
Light Middleweight—Boris Lagutin, Soviet Union.
Middleweight—Valery Popenchenko, Soviet Union.
Light Heavyweight—Cosimo Pinto, Italy.
Heavyweight—Joe Frazier, Philadelphia.

CANOEING
MEN'S EVENTS
Kayak Singles—Rolf Peterson, Sweden.
Kayak Doubles—Sven Sjodelius and Gunner Uttrberg, Sweden.
Kayak Fours—Soviet Union.
Canadian Singles—Jurgen Eschert, Germany.
Canadian Doubles—Andrei Khimich and Stepan Oschepov, Soviet Union.

WOMEN'S EVENTS
Kayak Singles—Ludmilla Khvedosiuk, Soviet Union.
Kayak Doubles—Roswitha Esser and Annemie Zimmerman, Germany.

CYCLING
Individual Road Race—Mario Zanin, Italy.
Road Team Time Trials—Netherlands.
1,000-Meter Time Trial—Patrick Sercu, Belgium.
1,000-Meter Scratch Giovanni Pettenella, Italy.
Individual Pursuit—Jiri Daller, Czechoslovakia.
Team Pursuit—Germany.
Tandem—Angelo Damiano and Sergio Bianchetto, Italy.

EQUESTRIAN
Three-Day Event Individual—Mauro Checcoli, Italy.
Three-Day Event, Team—Italy.
Dressage, Individual—Henri Chamartin, Switzerland.

10/1/64 — Arrival of Olympic torch in Tokyo is televised to U.S. via communications satellite Syncom III.

Dressage, Team—Germany.
Jumping, Individual—Jonquieres D-Oriola, France.
Jumping, Team—Germany.

FENCING
MEN'S EVENTS
Individual Foil—Egon Franke, Poland.
Team Foil—Soviet Union.
Individual Epee—Grigory Kriss, Soviet Union.
Team Epee—Hungary.
Individual Saber—Tubor Pezsa, Hungary.
Team Saber—Soviet Union.

WOMEN'S EVENTS
Individual Foil—Uldiko Ujlaki, Hungary.
Team Foil—Hungary.

JUDO
Lightweight—Takehide Nakatani, Japan.
Middleweight—Isao Okano, Japan.
Heavyweight—Isao Inokuma, Japan.
Open—Anton Geesink, Netherlands.

FIELD HOCKEY
Team—India.

GYMNASTICS
MEN'S EVENTS
Team—Japan.
All-Round—Yukio Endo, Japan.
Free Standing—Franco Menichelli, Italy.
Side Horse—Miroslav Cerar, Yugoslavia.
Flying Rings—Takuji Hayata, Japan.

Long Horse Vault—Haruhiro Yamashita, Japan.
Horizontal Bar—Boris Shakhlin, Soviet Union.
Parallel Bars—Endo.

WOMEN'S EVENTS
Team—Soviet Union.
All-Round—Vera Caslavaska, Czechoslovakia.
Free Standing—Larisa Latynina, Soviet Union.
Long Horse Vault—Vera Caslavska.
Uneven Parallel Bars—Polina Astakhova, Soviet Union.
Balance Beam—Vera Caslavska.

MODERN PENTATHLON
Individual—Ferenc Torok, Hungary.
Team—Soviet Union.

ROWING
Eight-Oared—Vesper Boat Club, Philadelphia.
Fours With Coxswain—Germany.
Fours Without Coxswain—Denmark.
Pairs With Coxswain—Stanford Crew Association (Conn Findlay, Belmont, Calif.; Ed Ferry Seattle; Kent Mitchell, Berkeley, Calif.)
Pairs Without Coxswain—Canada.
Double Sculls—Soviet Union.
Single Sculls—Vyacheslav Ivanov, Soviet Union.

SHOOTING
Free Rifle—Gary Anderson, Axtell, Neb.
Small-Bore Rifle (Three-Position) —Lones Wigger, Carter, Mont.

Small-Bore Rifle (Prone)—Laszlo Hammerl, Hungary.

Clay Pigeon—Ennio Matterelli, Italy.

Free Pistol—Vaino Markkanen, Finland.

Rapid-Fire Pistol—Pentti Linnosvuo, Finland.

SOCCER
Team—Hungary.

SWIMMING
MEN'S EVENTS
100-Meter Free-Style—Don Schollander, Lake Oswego, Ore., 0:53.4 (Olympic record; Steve Clark, Los Altos, Calif., tied world record of 0:52.9 on opening leg of 400-meter free-style relay.)

400-Meter Free-Style—Schollander, 4:12.2 (World record).

1,500-Meter Free-Stlye—Robert Windle, Australia, 17:01.7 (Olympic record).

200-Meter Breast Stroke—Ian O'Brien, Australia, 2:27.8 (World record).

200-Meter Butterfly—Kevin Berry, Australia, 2:06.6 (World record).

200-Meter Backstroke—Jed Graef, Verona, N.J., 2:10.3 (World record).

400-Meter Individual Medley—Dick Roth, Atherton, Calif., 4:45.4 (World record).

400-Meter Free-Style Relay—United States (Clark, Mike Austin, Rochester; Gary Ilman, San Jose, Calif.; Schollander), 3:32.2 (World record).

800-Meter Free-Style Relay—United States (Clark, Roy Saari, El Segundo, Calif.; Ilman, Schollander), 7:52.1 (World record).

400-Meter Medley Relay—United States (Thompson Mann, Chesapeake, Va.; Bill Craig, Glendale, Calif.; Fred Schmidt, Northbrook, Ill.; Clark), 3:58.4 (World record; Mann set world record of 0:59.6 for 100-meter backstroke on opening leg).

Springboard Dive—Ken Sitzberger, River Forest, Ill.

Platform Dive—Bob Webster, Santa Ana, Calif.

WOMEN'S EVENTS
100-Meter Free-Style—Dawn Fraser, Australia, 0:59.5 (Olympic record).

400-Meter Free Style—Ginny Duenkel, West Orange, N.J., 4:43.3 (Olympic record).

200-Meter Breast-Stroke—Galina Prazumenschikova, Soviet Union, 2:46.4 (Olympic record).

100-Meter Butterfly—Sharon Stouder, Glendora, Calif.; 1:04.7 (World record).

100-Meter Backstroke—Cathy Ferguson, Burbank, Calif., 1:07.7, (World record).

400-Meter Individual Medley—Donna de Varona, Santa Clara, Calif., 5:18.7 (Olympic record).

400-Meter Free-Style Relay—United States (Sharon Stouder, Donna de Varona, Pokey Watson, Potola Valley, Calif.; Kathy Ellis, Indianapolis), 4:03.8 (World record).

400-Meter Medley Relay—United States (Cathy Ferguson; Cynthia

10/14/64 — Marine Lt. Billy Mills, who is part Sioux, won 10,000 meter run, first American ever to take this event.

Goyette, Detroit; Sharon Stouder; Kathy Ellis), 4:33.9 (World record).

Springboard Dive—Mrs. Ingrid Kramer Engel, Germany.

Platform Dive—Lesley Bush, Princeton, N.J.

TRACK AND FIELD
MEN'S EVENTS
100-Meter Dash—Bob Hayes, Jacksonville, Fla., 0:10 (Equals world record).

200-Meter Dash—Henry Carr, Detroit, 0:23.3 (Olympic record).

400-Meter Run—Mike Larrabee, Fillmore, Calif., 0:45.1.

800-Meter Run—Peter Snell, New Zealand, 1:45.1 (Olympic record)

1,500-Meter Run—Snell, 3:38.1

5,000-Meter Run—Bob Schul, West Milton, Ohio, 13:48.8.

10,000-Meter Run—Billy Mills, Coffeyville, Kan., 28:24.4 (Olympic record).

Marathon—Abebe Bikila, Ethiop, 2:12:11 (World best).

110-Meter High Hurdles—Hayes Jones, Detroit, 0:13.6.

400-Meter Hurdles—Rex Cawley, Los Angeles, 0:49.6.

3,000-Meter Steeplechase—Gaston Roelants, Belgium, 8:30.8 (Olympic record).

20-Kilometer Walk—Ken Matthews Britain, 1:29:34.

50-Kilometer Walk—Abdon Pamich, Italy, 4:11:12.4 (World best).

400-Meter Relay—United States (Paul Drayton, Cleveland; Gerry Ashworth, Haverhill, Mass; Dick Stebbins, Los Angeles; Hayes), 0:39 (World record).

1,600-Meter Relay—United States (Ollan Cassell, Nutley, N.J.; Larrabee, Ulis Williams, Compton, Calif.; Carr), 3:00.7 (World record.

High Jump—Valery Brumel, Soviet Union, 7 feet 1 3/4 inches (Olympic record).

Pole Vault—Fred Hansen, Cuero, Tex. 16 feet 9 inches (Olympic record).

Broad Jump—Lynn Davies, Britain, 26 feet 5 1/2 inches.

Triple Jump—Joszef Schmidt, Poland, 55 feet 3 1/4 inches (Olympic record).

Shot-Put—Dallas Long, Los Angeles 66 feet 8 1/2 inches (Olympic record).

Discus Throw—Al Oerter, West Babylon, L.I., 200 feet 1 1/2 inches (Olympic record).

Hammer Throw—Romuald Klim, Soviet Union, 228 feet 10 1/2 inches (Olympic record).

10/27/64 — Even bigger surprise was provided by 17-year-old Lesley Bush, arriving home at far right, in 10-meter platform dive.

...4 — Biggest individual winner ...ng American athletes at Tokyo was 18-year-old swimmer Don Schollander of Oregon. He took four gold medals, in 100 and 400 meter freestyle and 400 and 800 meter relays.

Javelin Throw—Pauli Nevala, Finland, 271 feet 2 1/4 inches.
Decathlon—Willi Holdorf, Germany, 7,887 points.

WOMEN'S EVENTS

100-Meter Dash—Wyomia Tyus, Griffin, Ga., 0:11.4 (Miss Tyus equaled Olympic record of 0:11.3 in semi-finals).
200-Meter Dash—Edith McGuire, Atlanta, 0:23 (Olympic record).
400-Meter Run—Betty Cuthbert, Australia, 0:52 (Olympic record).
800-Meter Run—Ann Packer, Britain, 2:01.1 (World record).
80-Meter Hurdles—Karin Balzer, Germany, 0:10.5 (Equals world record).
400-Meter Relay—Poland, 0:43.6 (World record).
High Jump—Yolanda Balas, Rumania, 6 feet 2 3/4 inches (Olympic record).
Broad Jump—Mrs. Mary Rand, Britain, 22 feet 2 1/4 inches (World record).
Shot-Put—Tamara Press, Soviet Union, 59 feet 6 1/4 inches (Olympic record).
Discus Throw—Tamara Press, 187 feet 10 3/4 inches (Olympic record).
Javelin Throw—Mihaela Penes, Rumania, 198 feet 7 1/2 inches (Elena Gorchakova, Soviet Union set world record of 204—8 1/2 in qualifying round).
Pentathlon—Irina Press, Soviet Union, 5,246 points (World record).

VOLLEYBALL
Men's—Soviet Union.
Women's—Japan.

WATER POLO
Team—Hungary.

WEIGHT LIFTING
Bantamweight—Aleksi Vakhonin, Soviet Union, 786.5 pounds (World record).
Featherweight—Yoshinobu Miyake, Japan, 874.5 pounds (World record).
Lightweight—Waldemar Baszanowski, Poland, 951.5 pounds (Olympic record).
Middleweight—Hans Zdrazila, Czechoslovakia, 979 pounds

10/13/64 — America's Jed Graef, 22, pushes off on way to world record (2:10.3) in 200-meter backstroke.

10/21/64 — New Zealand's Peter Snell (466) on way to victory in 1,500 meter run. He also won 800.

mpic record).
ght Heavyweight–Rudolf Pluk-
felder, Soviet Union, 1,045
pounds (Olympic record).
Middle Heavyweight–Vladimir
Golovanov, Soviet Union,
1,072.5 pounds (World record).
Heavyweight–Leonid Zhabotinsky
Soviet Union, 1,259.5 pounds
(Olympic record).

WRESTLING
FREE-STYLE
Flyweight–Yoshikatsu Yoshida, Ja-
pan.
Bantamweight–Yojiru Uetake, Ja-
pan.
Featherweight–Osamu Wata-
nabe, Japan.
Lightweight–Enio Dimov, Bulgaria.
Welterweight–Ismail Ogan, Turk-
ey.
Middleweight–Prodan Gardjev,
Bulgaria.
Light Heavyweight–Aleksandr
Medved, Soviet Union.

Heavyweight–Aleksandr Ivanit-
sky, Soviet Union.

GRECO-ROMAN
Flyweight–Tsutomu Hanahara, Ja-
pan.
Bantamweight–Masamitsu Ichigu-
chi, Japan.
Featherweight–Imre Polyak, Hun-
gary.
Lightweight–Kazim Ayvas, Turkey
Welterweight–Anatoly Kolesov,
Soviet Union.
Middleweight–Branislav Simie
Yugoslavia.
Light Heavyweight–Bogan Alex-
androv. Bulgaria.
Heavyweight–Istvan Kozma, Hun-
gary.

YACHTING
5.5-Meter–Australia.
Dragon–Denmark.
Star–Bahamas.
Flying Dutchman–New Zealand.
Finn–Germany.

MEDAL STANDING

	G (1st)	S (2d)	B (3d)	T
United States...	36	26	28	90
Soviet Union...	30	31	35	96
Japan..............	16	5	8	29
Italy.................	10	10	6	26
Hungary..........	10	7	5	22
Germany..........	9	21	18	48
Poland.............	7	6	10	23
Australia.........	6	2	10	18
Czechoslovakia	5	6	3	14
Britain.............	4	12	1	17
Bulgaria..........	3	5	2	10
Finland............	3	0	2	5
New Zealand ..	3	0	2	5
Rumania..........	2	4	6	12
Netherlands.....	2	4	4	10
Turkey.............	2	3	1	6
Sweden............	2	2	4	8
Denmark..........	2	1	3	6
Yugoslavia.......	2	1	2	5
Belgium...........	2	0	1	3
Canada............	1	2	1	4
Switzerland	1	2	1	4
Ethiopia...........	1	0	0	1
Bahamas	1	0	0	1
India.................	1	0	0	1
France..............	0	7	6	13
Korea...............	0	2	1	3
Trinidad...........	0	1	2	3
Tunisia.............	0	1	1	2
Cuba.................	0	1	0	1
Argentina........	0	1	0	1
Pakistan...........	0	1	0	1
Philipines	0	1	0	1
Iran..................	0	0	2	2
Ireland.............	0	0	1	1
Kenya...............	0	0	1	1
Mexico.............	0	0	1	1
Brazil...............	0	0	1	1
Ghana..............	0	0	1	1
Nigeria............	0	0	1	1
Uruguay...........	0	0	1	1
Total..............	161	165	172	498

10/15/64 – Segregation ruled in Olympic Village as
wire fence separated women athletes from men.

295

10/16/64 — America's world-record setting women's 400-meter freestyle team after winning at Tokyo. From left to right they are Donna de Varona, Lillian Watson, Cathy Ellis and Sharon Stroudern

10/23/64 — America maintained perfect record in Olympic basketball, winning every game, including final against Russia. Brazil finished third.

10/21/64 — Ulis Williams of U.S. falls to track after passing baton to Henry Carr in 1,600 meter relay. Carr, who won 200 meter gold medal, anchored Americans to world record victory.

10/23/64 — White-shirted Czech player out-maneuvers three Hungarians in Olympic soccer final but to no avail. Hungarians won game, 2-1, and took gold medal.

10/22/64 — America's Francine Fox and Gloriane Perrier (at left) brought unexpected silver medal to U.S. in woman's kayak pairs. German girls finished first while Romanians were third.

10/14/64 — Cathy Ferguson of U.S. (bottom), France's Christine Caron and America's Ginny Duenkel in "wet" blanket finish of 100-meter backstroke. Cathy won.

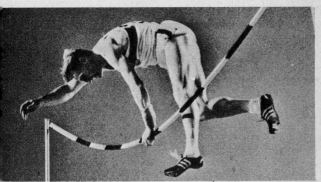

10/23/64 — Germany's Wolfgang Reinhardt tries to hoist himself over bar in pole vault event which lasted nine hours. He was second to America's Fred Hansen.

10/16/64 — Surprise winner in women's 100-meter dash was Wyomia Tyus (right), 19, of Tennessee State.

"MY FAIR LADY" - WORLD PREMIER

10/22/64 — Broadway's most successful musical comedy, "My Fair Lady," caused even bigger uproar when world premiere of film version was held in New York. Traffic was jammed for 14 blocks, forcing many celebrities to walk to theatre. Among those who caught crowd's eye were (top photo) Rex Harrison, star of both stage and screen versions with Sybil Burton; Audrey Hepburn (second photo) who plays Eliza Doolittle in film, with husband Mel Ferrer; movie mogul Jack Warner (third photo, left) with composer Frederick Lowe and lyricist Alan Lerner, the pair who set "Pygmalion" to music; and (bottom photo) Gloria Vanderbilt with husband Wyatt Cooper. On Broadway, show ran for 2,717 performances, a musical record, and topped only by "Life With Father" (3,182) and "Tobacco Road" (3,182). Movie cost $17 million, but most critics felt it worth the expense.

ENTERTAINMENT, SPORTS & THE ARTS

10/22/64 — Eye-popping sight at premiere was that of actress Monique Van Vooren.

10/22/64 — Mrs. Stephen Smith, sister of late Pres. Kennedy, was there, too.

WORLD SERIES

10/19/64 — World Series produced raft of heroes, but at end the biggest was St. Louis Cardinal pitcher Bob Gibson, who at right with his wife, picks up keys to sports car he won as outstanding player. He won two games, set strikeout record as Cards won over Yankees in seven games. Others who excelled were Yanks' Mickey Mantle (below), who hit three homers, and Cards' Tim Mc-Carver, who batted .478.

299

10/23/64 — Series had odd windup as winning manager Johnny Keane (above) resigned post with Cardinals and was then hired by Yanks to replace Yogi Berra (right), who had won American League pennant in his first year.

10/16/64 — Speed records took a beating at Utah's Bonneville Salt Flats. Craig Breedlove's three-wheeled "Spirit of America" (top left) was first vehicle to top 500 mph on land, averaging 526.26 on two runs through the measured mile. When Breedlove tried to slow down, car went out of control, crashed in canal. Two weeks later, Art Arfons' "Green Monster" hit 571.? mph despite flat tire.

10/26/64 — Minnesota Viking defensive end Jim Marshall indicates direction he should have run in pro grid game. He picked up fumble, ran ? yards to wrong end zone.

10/9/64 — High-flying member of Russia's Moiseyev Dance Company goes into orbit over Commie chorus line in performance in London.

10/5/64 .— Bespectacled film stars George C. Scott and Ava Gardner take stroll in Rome where they are playing Abraham and Sarah in film version of "The Bible."

10/13/64 —Actress May Britt, wife of Sammy Davis Jr., plays perfect hostess and listens attentively to Elizabeth Taylor at party given in New York City.

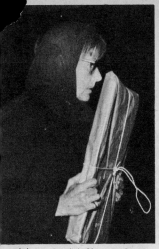

10/7/64 — Swedish film star Greta Garbo arrives in New York for funeral of long-time friend George Schlee.

10/8/64 — Sculptor Edmund Kara inspects redwood statue M-G-M commissioned him to do of Elizabeth Taylor.

10/7/64 — John Wayne, with wife, leaves Calif. hospital after operation.

10/24/64 — Carroll Baker dazzles fans at premiere of "The Carpetbaggers."

MIGRATION

10/16/64 – As cold approaches, swarm of migratory birds heads South from Iowa cornfield.

10/21/64 – Leon Gillis, 43, ginia, leads covered wagon contain.. ing his wife and children into Moscow, completing six-week journey across Russia. He wanted to personally meet Nikita Khrushchev, but was too late. Though he arrived days after Soviet leader was replaced, no one along way told him so.

10/22/64 – Danish couple enjoy pleasant luncheon-out in Copenhagen on trolley car. New policy allows citizens to hire trolley for personal use at cost of $27 for 90 minutes. Service includes driver, two conductors and freedom to go anywhere on the trolley line.

10/6/64 – Dr. Walter Robb of General Electric Laboratory in Schenectady, N.Y., keeps watchful eye on mouse which is breathing air while encased in special "gill" cage he invented. Cage, submerged in water, is made of silicone membrane that allows oxygen from water to filter through.

10/28/64 – Dr. Jerome Weiss uses plastic replica of human stomach to demonstrate new diagnostic tool, called the Intragastric Camera, in New York. Tiny camera, with 16 lenses, flash bulb, is attached to rubber tube, takes internal pictures.

OCTOBER – END

SUMMARY-NOVEMBER 1964

NATIONAL

President **Lyndon B. Johnson** as predicted by the polls buried Senator Barry Goldwater in an avalanche of votes in the national elections (Nov. 3). The President received more than 41 million votes to the Senator's 26 million, the plurality of better than 15 million being the largest in history. The winner took 45 of 50 states and rolled up 485 electoral votes to Goldwater's 52. LBJ's landslide victory produced important Democratic gains in Congress particularly in the House of Representatives and enabled **Robert Kennedy,** brother of the late President John F. Kennedy, to win a decisive victory over Senator Kenneth Keating in the contest for U.S. Senate in New York. In Ohio, the Johnson landslide resulted in the unexpected victory of incumbent **Stephen Young over Robert A. Taft Jr.** for the Senate seat from that state. In New York, the Democrats won control of the state legislature for the first time in 35 years.

Despite their defeat, Conservative Republicans announced (Nov. 13) that they would fight to retain **Dean Burch** as National Chairman of the Republican Party.

Local strikes involving 25,000 workers in Ford Motor Company plants (Nov. 5) crippled production and brought about the layoff of 33,000 additional employees by Nov. 12; but on Nov. 23, the Company and the Union signed a new three-year contract resolving the dispute.

The worst drought in history created conditions in the North-east United States causing fires and water shortages throughout the area.

Secretary of Defense Robert S. McNamara announced (Nov. 18) plans for closing 95 military installations in 33 states and five foreign countries involving 63,000 military and civilian jobs......**The Federal Reserve Bank** raised the bank discount rate from 3.5% to 4% in response to a rise in the British rate from 5 to 7% ......**President Johnson** said (Nov. 17) that he would ask the new Congress to give priority to **medical care for the aged** and aid to Appalachia.

Six hundred and fifty whites in McComb, Miss., a center of racial conflict, issued an appeal for an end to racial violence and for equal treatment for all under the law......**J. Edgar Hoover,** Director of the Federal Bureau of Investigation called (Nov. 18) the Warren Report on the assassination of President John F. Kennedy unfair in its criticism of the FBI. In the same statement Hoover labeled **Negro Civil Rights leader Dr. Martin Luther King** "the most notorious liar in the country" for saying that Georgia FBI agents failed to act in civil rights cases......**A news**

magazine reported (Nov. 29) that President Johnson was seeking a replacement for Hoover as head of the FBI. The report was denied by the White House.

Rare Greek manuscripts allegedly stolen 20 years ago from Spain turned up in the library of Yale University. The dealer who sold the mss to Yale claimed that church officials in Spain had disposed of them in order to raise funds for the repair of Saragossa Cathedral......**The New York Police Department** officially cleared (Nov. 16) Lt. Thomas Gilligan of all blame in the shooting of a 15-year-old Negro boy which triggered the July riots in Harlem and Brooklyn......**A group of socially prominent Connecticut parents** were fined for supplying liquor to teen-agers at private parties......**A 72-year-old Oklahoma Supreme Court Justice, Earl Welch,** was fined and sentenced to three years in prison for evading taxes between 1957-61 ......**The Federal Communications Commission** (FCC) reopened the 1960 investigation of bribery in radio and TV which had revealed widespread payoffs to disc jockeys and fixed quiz shows......**In Florida,** a Federal Grand Jury decided that **cigarettes are reasonably safe** and fit for human consumption in a suit by the estate of a man who had died of lung cancer in 1957 and who had smoked three packages of cigarettes a day for 30 years......**An FBI report** disclosed that crime in the suburbs had risen substantially more than in the nation as a whole.

The U.S. successfully launched a space vehicle to probe conditions on the planet Mars. **The Soviet Union** launched a similar probe two days later.

INTERNATIONAL

Communist forces staged (Nov. 1) a successful attack on the U.S. air base just north of Saigon in South Viet Nam. Four Americans were killed, five bombers destroyed and 22 other planes damaged......**U.S. Ambassador to S. Viet Nam Maxwell D. Taylor** was reported favoring extension of war to North Viet Nam......**Vietnamese Premier Tran Van Huong** imposed virtual martial law as students and Buddhists rioted against his government (Nov. 25).

President Victor Paz Estenssoro of Bolivia fled the country after a successful military revolt against his regime. He was succeeded by Vice-President, General Rene Barrientos......**With the ratification** (Nov. 17) of an extradition treaty between the U.S. and Brazil, that country ended its long history as a haven for U.S. fugitives from justice.

Premier Chou En-lai of Red China led a delegation to Moscow (Nov. 5) ostensibly for the celebration of the 47th anniversary of the Russian Revolution but in reality, according to experts, to discuss with the new Russian rulers the differences between the two countries......**Russia postponed** (Nov. 11) indefinitely the previously called world conference of Communist parties in what was interpreted as a conciliatory gesture towards Red China......**Aleksei Adzhubei,** son-in-law of deposed Russian ruler Nikita Khrushchev, was expelled from the Central Committee of the Communist Party. He was replaced by **N. Shelepin who emerged as "a man to watch"** for the future.

Finance Minister Eisaku Sato was chosen to succeed ailing Hagato Ikeda as Premier of Japan......After ruling for 45 years, the 68-year-old **Grand Duchess Charlotte** of Luxembourg stepped down in favor of 45-year-old Crown Prince Jean ......Goodwill messages from all over the world hailed **Winston Churchill,** Britain's wartime Prime Minister, on the occasion of his 90th birthday (Nov. 30).

Border warfare broke out between Syria and Israel. Both sides accused the other in the United Nations of starting the conflict......**Britain embargoed all arms shipments to South Africa**......**Belgian paratroopers** in U.S. planes dropped into Stanleyville in the Congo to rescue white hostages held by forces in rebellion against Premier Tshombe. African nations and Communist countries protested the action with violent demonstrations against U.S. embassies.

In Rome, two officials were charged with having kidnaped and trying to ship a bound, gagged and drugged Israeli citizen to Cairo in a crate sent as diplomatic baggage.

After 18 months of haggling over rules, The Kennedy Round tariff negotiators got down to serious business in Geneva (Nov. 16)......**Eleven nations subscribed (Nov. 25) to a three billion dollar loan to Britain** to save the pound from devaluation.

Pope Paul VI donated a three-tiered jeweled tiara to the poor of the world......**Catholic Bishops** in Rome, by a vote of 2099-46, affirmed their right to share rule of the Church with the Pope......**The Ecumenical Council** approved (Nov. 20) a document condemning anti-semitism and asserting that the Jews bore no special guilt in the crucifixion of Christ.

SPORTS

Gene Mauch, of the Philadelphia Phillies, was voted Manager of the Year ......**Brooks Robinson** of the Baltimore Orioles named Most Valuable Player in the American League......**Ken Boyer** of the World's Champions St. Louis Cards was voted Most Valuable Player in the National League.

    Sudden surgery (Nov. 13) forced **Cassius Clay** to postpone the defense of his World Heavyweight title against Sonny Liston scheduled for November 16.

    Peter Snell set a new world's record for the mile with a mark of 3.54:1.

OBITUARIES

Roy Wilson Howard, Chairman of the Board of the Scripps-Howard Newspapers (N.Y. World-Telegram etc.), aged 81 in New York.

William O'Dwyer, Irish immigrant who rose from ordinary patrolman in the New York police force to become Mayor of the city and later Ambassador to Mexico, aged 74 in New York.

11/4/64 — With nation's votes corralled, it's round-up time at the LBJ ranch.

NATIONAL ELECTIONS

11/3/64 — With most public opinion polls predicting President Lyndon B. Johnson would win 60 to 64 per cent of the popular vote, but with Senator Barry Goldwater conceding only five states, America went to the polls on the first Tuesday following the first Monday in November and settled the issue. Some 42.1 million Americans cast their votes for the President and his Democratic running mate, Senator Hubert H. Humphrey, the largest number to back a presidential slate since General Dwight D. Eisenhower collected 35.5 million votes in 1956. The Johnson landslide (a record 61.3 per cent) swept many Democrats into office around the country as he carried 44 states and rolled up 486 electoral votes to 52 for Goldwater. The Arizona Republican ran behind many state and local tickets as he polled some eight million votes less than Richard M. Nixon did in 1960. As a party, Republicans suffered a net loss of two seats in the Senate and 39 in the House of Representatives, but actually gained one state governorship (even though losing 17 of 25 races). Analysis of votes showed nation rejected Senator Goldwater's stands on civil rights, economic issues and foreign policy.

11/3/64 — Negro voters go to the polls in Harlem to cast ballots in presidential election. In some precincts President Johnson won 99 per cent of the Negro vote.

11/4/64 — Senator Goldwater waves in Phoenix after making concession speech.

11/4/64 — Senator Edward Kennedy, in Mass. hospital, easily won re-election.

11/4/64 — Despite Johnson sweep in Michigan, Republican Gov. George Romney, with wife, scored stunning victory.

11/5/64 — Sen. and Mrs. Stephen Young of Ohio return to Washington after he upset Republican Robert Taft Jr.

11/3/64 – One of the nation's mo[st] publicized election races involved Robert F. Kennedy (at left with son David at election-eve rally) and Senator Kenneth Keating in New York. Mr. Kennedy, the former Attorney General and brother of the late President, survived "carpetbagger" issue, a reference to his Massachusetts background, to unseat Keating, a popular Republican, who ran well ahead of Goldwater-Miller ticket, but couldn't overcome Johnson landslide which amounted to 68.2 per cent of vote in New York. Thus, Kennedy family became first to send three men of one generation to the Senate. Election map (below) shows state-by-state results of electoral vote.

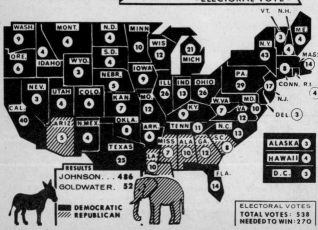

PRESIDENTIAL ELECTION 1964 ★ELECTORAL VOTE★

State	Electoral Votes
WASH.	9
ORE.	6
MONT.	4
IDAHO	4
WYO.	3
N.D.	4
S.D.	4
NEBR.	5
MINN.	10
WIS.	12
IOWA	9
MICH.	21
VT.	3
N.H.	4
ME.	4
N.Y.	43
MASS	14
NEV.	3
UTAH	4
COLO.	6
KAN.	7
MO.	12
ILL.	26
IND.	13
OHIO	26
PA.	29
CONN.	8
R.I.	4
CAL.	40
ARIZ.	5
N.MEX.	4
OKLA.	8
ARK.	6
KY.	9
W.VA.	7
VA.	12
MD.	10
N.J.	17
DEL.	3
TEXAS	25
TENN.	11
N.C.	13
MISS	7
ALA.	10
GA.	12
S.C.	8
LA.	10
FLA.	14
ALASKA	3
HAWAII	4
D.C.	3

RESULTS
JOHNSON... **486**
GOLDWATER. **52**

■ DEMOCRATIC
▨ REPUBLICAN

ELECTORAL VOTES
TOTAL VOTES: 538
NEEDED TO WIN: 270

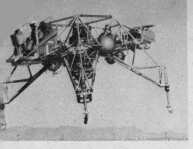

11/6/64 – Experimental moon landing vehicle undergoes tests at Edwards Air Force base in Calif. National Aeronautics and Space Administration is using vehicle to study piloting and operational procedures involved in a manned lunar landing.

11/9/64 – Mrs. Edward Kennedy, wife of Democratic Senator, admires an exhibit at Kennedy Library Museum in Dublin, Ireland. Irish President and Mrs. Eamon de Valera join Mrs. Kennedy at opening of the memorial to the late U.S. President.

11/9/64 – Thirteen-month-old Todd Klemz is held in arms of nurse Sharon Rohr as Dr. Karel Absolon looks on in Minneapolis after Todd was subject of first liver graft in history. Dr. Absolon headed team of doctors which took healthy liver from a dead child and transferred it to Todd in 36-minute operation.

11/10/64 – Officials in Fitchburg, Mass., survey scene which was becoming all too typical throughout New England and Mid-Atlantic states; namely a severely depleted reservoir. Seven-month long drought dropped level of Fitchburg reservoir 12 ft.; officials said dry spell was worst in 177 years.

11/13/64 — Rep. Adam Clayton Powell relaxes in Waikiki lounge in Honolulu with his secretary, Miss C. A. Huff, just minutes before Harlem Congressman allegedly threatened to "slug" a newspaperman.

11/19/64 — Statue of Liberty salutes, or so it appears, new Verrazano Bridge, largest suspension span in U.S.

11/13/64 — Carolyn Mignini, 17, of Baltimore, flashes winning smile in Dallas as Miss Teenage America.

11/17/64 — Vonda Van Dyke, Miss America of 1965, huddles with four-year-old Mickey Heinicke, 1965 National March of Dimes child, in New York. They are both touring the nation.

11/15/64 — Pilot's cap, severed tail section, rest silently in snow on Nevada mountain-top where 29 died as airliner crashed in storm.

11/19/64 – Col. John Glenn, first American to orbit the earth, prepares for his first solo flight since receiving head injury last February. His sense of balance was affected by a fall, but Marine doctors gave him "clean bill of health." Though he plans to retire from Corps in January, he intends to keep flying in civilian life.

11/20/64 – After 163 years of building the ships in which U.S. sailors have gone down to the sea, Brooklyn Navy Yard (left) was ordered shut down by Defense Secretary Robert McNamara. Pentagon economy plans also called for closing of 94 other military bases, saving government $477 million annually.

11/19/64 – U.S. Marine Corps unveiled world's fastest (200 mph) and most powerful helicopter at Stratford, Conn. The craft, called the Sikorsky CH-53A, will be able to carry nine tons of cargo.

11/19/64 – Relaxing after rigorous political campaign, U.S. Vice President-elect Hubert H. Humphrey romps between boulders on beach at Little Dix Bay on Virgin Gorda in the British Virgin Islands, where he and Mrs. Humphrey went on a side-trip while vacationing at U.S. owned St. John Island.

11/22/64 — Robert F. Kennedy kneels before eternal flame in Arlington, Va., marking grave of his brother John F. Kennedy on first anniversary of his assassination.

11/29/64 — Cleveland Williams, leading contender for the heavyweight boxing championship, lies in Houston hospital bed after five-hour operation. Williams was shot during a scuffle with a highway patrolman who arrested him for drunken driving.

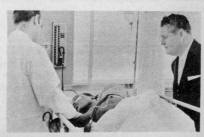

THE CONGO

11/14/64 — White mercenary eyes rebel movements across Congo's Lualaba River.

Success of Premier Moise Tshombe's Congolese Army, led by white officers and mercenaries recruited from South Africa and Rhodesia, against rebel forces triggered international incident when insurgents threatened to massacre white hostages in Stanleyville. U.S. and Belgium reacted by announcing airlift of Belgian paratroopers (in American planes) from Ascenscion Island, a British possession. As Congolese forces closed in on Stanleyville, air drop was executed with paratroopers arriving just as rebels began firing indiscriminately at hundreds of hostages, including women and children, in the downtown area.

...64 — Congolese soldiers hustled bound rebel prisoner aboard plane at Kindu in The Congo. One of several rebel leaders captured by advancing government troops, man was flown to Leopoldville to stand trial for atrocities committed at Kindu.

11/24/64 — Belgian paratrooper bends over body of Dr. Paul Carlson, an American missionary, in Stanleyville. Sentenced to death by rebels for supposedly spying, Carlson won reprieve only to be shot — by chance — when rebels fired upon 250 hostages, killing 29.

11/24/64 — Among those rescued at Stanleyville was U.S. Consul Michael Hoyt (center) talking here with newsmen in Leopoldville. Rebels threatened to kill him, forced him and other U.S. officials to eat an American flag.

11/24/64 — Congo Premier Moise Tshombe, who consented to U.S.-Belgian airlift, greets first group of rescued hostages to arrive at Leopoldville. More than 700 whites were saved from rebels.

11/26/64 — White mercenary attached to Congolese Army gives aid to wounded rebel as fighting continues in Stanleyville. Next day, Belgian paratroopers were withdrawn as criticism—mostly by African and Communist nations—mounted. Air drop was denounced as "imperialist intervention," but President Lyndon Johnson defended it as a humanitarian move.

11/30/64 — Cruel and unexpected aftermath of Congo rescue mission took place upon Belgian paratroopers' return to Brussels. Mrs. Lucien Welvaert (spotted coat) went to greet her husband at airport, then collapsed when told he had been killed. His name had not been included on casualty lists, but another paratrooper, named Didier Welvaert, had mistakenly been listed as among the dead.

.¡/4/64 — Ousted Bolivian President Victor Paz Estenssoro walks hand-in-hand with two of his daughters following arrival in Lima, Peru. One-day military rebellion, led by General Alfredo Obandio Candia, forced Dr. Paz, who had been in power for 12 years, to flee country. Army Junta replaced him with Vice President Rene Barrientos, who reportedly had hand in coup.

11/1/64 — Turbo fan (arrow, below) is last recognizable part of U.S. B-57 jet bomber, destroyed by Viet Cong guerrillas in surprise attack on top-secret Bien Hoa Air Base, South Viet Nam. Four Americans died.

11/2/64 — Elderly East German mother embraces her daughter in Frankfurt, West Germany after taking special train from East Germany. She was in first group permitted to leave Communist territory since Berlin Wall was constructed three years ago.

11/3/64 — Wearing the Imperial Crown, a dazzling white lace gown and the scarlet coronation robe trimmed with white ermine, Queen Elizabeth II lends note of enchantment to traditional ceremony of the State Opening of Parliament in London. Lords preceding her carry Cap of Maintenance and (at right) the Sword of State.

11/8/64 — Reacting much like a proud father-to-be, King Constantine of Greece holds hands with his Danish-born wife, Queen Anne Marie, at announcement in Florina that 18-year-old Queen was expecting to give birth to her first baby next June.

11/9/64 — Eisaku Sato (right), 63-year-old Liberal Democrat, receives congratulations of Socialist Party chairman Jyotaro Eawakami after being elected Premier of Japan. Sato, a pro-Westerner, hopes to project Japan into larger role in world affairs, may step up trade with Red China.

11/10/64 — Honor guard receives Zero fighter plane in Tokyo after it was formally presented to Japan by U.S. Found years ago on Guam, it was rebuilt, presented as goodwill gift. It is only Zero left.

11/11/64 — Two British Airmen, out to conquer Mawenzi Peak, twin to the famed Mt. Kilimanjaro in Kenya, came upon nine-year-old wreckage of East African Airways flight which disappeared. Plane apparently slammed into face of mountain at 15,000 feet. All aboard the DC-3 were lost, but plane's tires were still inflated.

11/12/64 — Grand Duke Pierre takes oath of fidelity upon becoming new ruler of Luxembourg. His wife, Grand Duchess Josephine-Charlotte, and son, Prince Jean, look on. His mother, the Grand Duchess Charlotte, abdicated after 45-year reign.

11/12/64 – Members of left-wing "Zengakuren" student group use bamboo poles to attack police in Tokyo demonstration protesting visit of U.S. atomic sub.

11/13/64 – Member of Israeli "kib-butz" along Syrian border clears away rubble after clash between armed forces of two nations. Israeli jets attacked Syrian gun positions after Syrians opened fire on Israel border settlement. Bullet-scarred walls attest to fury of the exchange.

11/16/64 – Helping hand at right is given to Communist Chinese boss Mao Tze-tung in Peiping and is captured by French cameraman working for CBS. Red China's leader had been helped to speaker's platform by aides and photo was taken without knowledge of Communist officials.

11/16/64 – Eight years after bloody revolution in the streets of Budapest, Hungarian citizens linger at sidewalk cafe on banks of Danube, a scene most untypical of Red world.

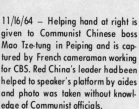

11/16/64 — Back-to-back typhoons, followed monsoon rains, drove more than a million South Vietnamese from their homes, inundated up to 90 per cent of some provinces, forced these villagers to barbecue dogs to avert starvation.

11/17/64 — Egyptian Embassy officials in Rome were thwarted in attempt to smuggle Joseph Dahan (right) in trunk (left) aboard flight to Cairo. Dahan, found alive, turned out to be an Israeli, was suspected of being a double agent.

11/17/64 — Senator-elect Robert Kennedy and Mexican President Adolfo Lopez Mateos unveil plaque dedicating 3,000-apartment housing unit in Mexico City after the late U.S. President John F. Kennedy. The $10-million development, an Alliance for Progress project, was financed by American trade union movement.

11/19/64 — Panama's President Marco Robles talks to students demanding ouster of government officials opposed to scrapping 61-year-old treaty with U.S. concerning Panama Canal. Four days later it took more than words to calm students. They conducted demonstration outside Legislative Palace as National Assembly held secret session delving into administration's conduct of relations with United States. National Guardsmen used tear gas and rifle shots (over heads of crowd) to quell the disturbance.

11/22/64 — Policemen and paratroopers, using bamboo shields to ward off rocks thrown by demonstrators in Saigon, "return fire" as new wave of disturbances hits South Viet Nam capital.

11/26/64 — "Kennedy" Library at American Embassy in Cairo is gutted by fire after African students wrecked offices and ignited furniture in protest against U.S.-Belgian mercy mission in The Congo. Similar demonstrations took place in other African nations and also in Iron Curtain countries.

11/28/64 — Newsman's car goes up in flames outside U.S. Embassy in Moscow as mounted policemen drive back angry student demonstrators. Rock-throwing mobs of Africans and Russians stormed U.S., Belgian and British embassies in protest against Congo rescue mission.

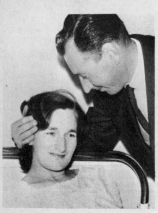

11/23/64 — French postman Raymond Sambor congratulates his wife Monique, 27, in hospital near Paris after she gave birth to quintuplets, Europe's first.

11/29/64 — Ana Olga Capestany, 19-year-old Cuban, poses in West Palm Beach after she leaped off Cuban-bound ship. Coast Guard picked her up.

11/26/64 — Seaman from Norwegian tanker Stolt Dagali is led to quarters aboard Israeli cruise liner Shalom after the latter, outward bound on Caribbean cruise, sliced through the tanker in heavy fog off New Jersey coast. Stern section of Norwegian ship sank immediately; 13 crew members drowned in ocean.

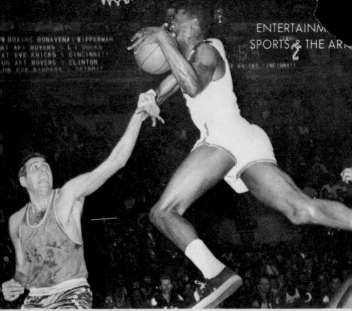

11/14/64 — Boston's all-time NBA-great Bill Russell drives for basket in Madison Square Garden, but Philadelphia's Al Bianchi "handles" him . . . illegally.

11/20/64 — Heavyweight champion Cassius Clay (in wheelchair), with wife Sonji at his side, meets press in Boston hospital for first time since undergoing hernia operation which forced cancellation of title bout with Sonny Liston.

11/13/64 — Seven-year-old Bedri Baykam of Turkey poses in front of one of his drawings in Paris. Shielded from press by his parents, the amazing art prodigy, whose work has been compared to Matisse, has drawn 3,500 pictures.

11/21/64 — Win-wacky Wolverines of Michigan whoop it up after whipping Ohio State, 10-0, and winning trip to the Rose Bowl.

ptery of Chimney Rock

	7½
Kingman	29
Lola	17
Diana	17
Paula	25
Don	4

NIL
Lola
Diana
James Bond

11/25/64 — ''Ben Franklin In Paris'' had nothing on Vice President-elect Hubert Humphrey backstage in New York.

329

11/19/64 – Spanish Matador Emilio Olivia, having planted three banderillas in bull, finds himself on wrong end of the punishment in Caracas, Venezuela. Though apparently on way to easy victory, Olivia wound up with 20 stitches in leg.

11/12/64 – Visitor at African art exhibition at Arts Decoratif Museum in Paris (opposite page) views unique wood carving done by member of Bangwa Tribe.

11/5/64 — Johnny Keane, who managed St. Louis Cards to World Series win, then quit to manage N.Y. Yankees—the team he beat—is named NL manager of year.

11/17/64 — Yogi Berra, fired after managing Yanks to AL pennant, poses in front of Shea Stadium after accepting post as coach with New York Mets.

11/30/64 — China Machado, fashion editor of Harper's Bazaar magazine, dances at Far Eastern Pageant in N.Y. Metropolitan Museum of Art.

11/12/64 — England's Ann Sydney, 20-year-old hair stylist, wins Miss World title in 41-nation competition at London's Lyceum Ballroom.

11/25/64 — Thirteen-year-old Frankie Dees kicks up wall of water while taking sharp turn in winning junior water ski championship at Cypress Gardens, Fla.

11/30/64 — It happens every fall, the selection of All-America football teams. UPI's 1964 college honor team included two Notre Dame players, end Jack Snow and quarterback John Huarte, and two players from U. of Illinois, fullback Jim Grabow-ski and center Dick Butkus; plus backs Gale Sayers, Kansas, and Jerry Rhome, Tulsa; end Larry Elkins, Baylor; tackles Larry Kramer, Nebraska, and Ralph Neely, Oklahoma; and guards Rick Redman, Washington, and Tommy Nobis, Texas.

11/12/64 — Red Chinese boss Mao Tze-tung joins other Communist Party leaders in applauding, on stage, the dancers of China's first modern ballet company after Peking performance of "The Red Detachment of Women." Reviews were favorable, which figures.

11/12/64 — Europe's top male actor Alain Delon meets America's Ann-Margret on Hollywood set.

11/25/64 – Designer Rose Marie's answer to controversial topless bathing suit is a jewelled, peek-a-boo number called "Mystique."

11/30/64 – University of Southern California students stage protest bonfire after grid Trojans, who upset previously unbeaten Notre Dame the day before, were by-passed by Rose Bowl committee, who picked Oregon State to meet Michigan.

ENTERTAINMENT, SPORTS & THE ARTS–END   335

11/19/64 — A 6-billion-to-one was caught by camera in Middletown, N.Y., and, if the phenomenon escapes you, that's one egg (perfectly formed) inside another, plus a normal yoke. Some six billion eggs are laid each year and yet fewer than one double egg is found . . . yet the very next day, another yoke-within-a-yoke was found in the same barnyard.

11/2/64 — When Thomas Jefferson was President of the United States, back in 1805, the spry old chap at left was, supposedly, born in Russia. That makes Shiraly Muslimov, seen here with a great-great- etc-grandson, something like 159 years old.

MISCELLANY

11/17/64 — The old theme of "boy-meets-girl, boy-wins-girl, boy-loses-girl" took on sinister, and quite literal, meaning in Germany. The plot went this way: Dorthea Voss, 18 (top photo with her father), met, and married, 26-year-old Peter Selle (bottom photo, with police guard) in West Germany. Peter was refugee from East Germany, but what Dorthea didn't know was that she closely resembled the 24-year-old wife Pete left behind. Once wed, Pete suggested trip behind Iron Curtain. He promptly ditched Dorthea, lifting her identification papers in process. He then took wife No. 1 to West Germany. Meanwhile Dorthea spent six weeks in Red jail trying to prove her identity. She did, and Pete was tried for kidnaping.

11/12/64 – The smile of a boy as he hugs his dog can mean many things, but this one is something special. The fellow with the tooth missing is James (Bucky) Welch and the dog is Smokey, who in August somehow got caught beneath a freight train in Louisville. Bucky crawled under the train to rescue his friend, and the train started up. The seven-year-old youngster lost both his arms, but survived. Now he's ready to be fitted with artificial limbs, while Smokey, well, he looks like he's had enough of this picture-stuff; he wants a walk in the park with Buc ...let's make it... Plucky.

11/7/64 – Global cooperation is not always a headline affair. Here pretty, 21-year-old Beatrice Maberry of Richland, Wash., takes time from her chores to pose with her "host mother" Mrs. Kaspar Hahn in field near Holzkirchen, West Germany. Hahns are one of five families Bea has lived and worked with in past six months under the International Farm Youth Exchange (IFYE) program, one of the oldest and most successful two-way exchange programs in existence.

11/17/64 — Broadening base solves the battle of the bulge on the boardwalk at Atlantic City.

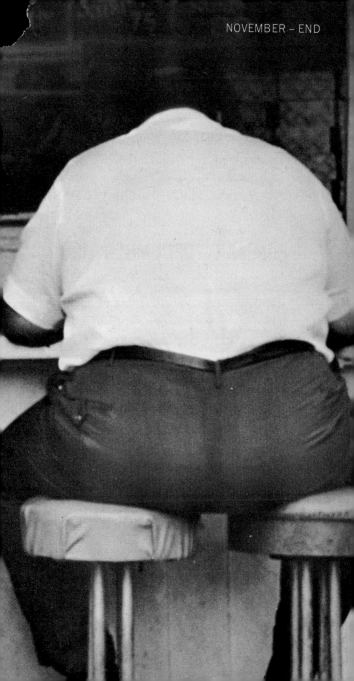

SUMMARY - DECEMBER 1964

NATIONAL

A **Federal court** ruled that grants by a state to all-white private schools were a transparent evasion of the 14th Amendment . . . . **J. Raymond Jones** was elected leader of New York County Democrats, the first Negro in history to hold a post that used to be better known as 'Boss of Tammany Hall' . . . . **The Federal Bureau of Investigation (FBI)** arrested (Dec. 4) 21 white men in Mississippi on a charge of violating civil rights in connection with the murder of two white and one Negro civil rights workers in Mississippi in June. Charges were dismissed by a U.S. Commissioner (Dec. 10). . . . **President Lyndon B. Johnson** approved the withdrawal of Federal aid from states and cities that discriminate against Negroes in federally financed projects . . . **The U.S. Supreme Court** voided (Dec. 7) a Florida law which penalizes sexual relations between whites and non-whites . . . . President Johnson named **Vice President-elect Hubert H. Humphrey** to coordinate all Government 'Equal Opportunity' programs . . . . **The U.S. Supreme Court** unanimously upheld (Dec. 14) the public accommodations section of the Civil Rights Act of 1964. By a vote of 5-4, the Court ruled that the Act wiped out all pending state prosecutions for peaceful demonstrations against discrimination in public accommodations . . . . **Five Mississippi whites** who pleaded guilty to participating in racial bombings were fired from their jobs with the Illinois Central Railroad.

An 11-man special board urged (Dec. 1) the American Medical Association to abandon its historic hands-off policy on birth control and sexual behavior to sponsor educational programs in both areas . . . . **Columbia University's School of Dentistry** was deprived of full accreditation by the American Dental Association . . . . **Notre Dame University** successfully sued for an injunction to prevent the showing of a 20th-Century-Fox film, "John Goldfarb, Please Come Home" alleging that the film invades the University's privacy and depicts its football team as 'drunks and gluttons'. The film cost $4 million. The injunction also applied to two books with the same title . . . . **For the first time in television history,** the three networks were tied in the national ratings issued on December 6 . . . . **Police arrested** (Dec. 3) 786 students of the University of California at Berkeley staging a sit-in to protest 'restrictions on free speech'.

Senator Barry M. Goldwater ruled himself out (Dec. 14) as a future presidential candidate . . . . A survey reported (Dec. 17) that only one fifth of registered Republicans want Senator Goldwater to remain as head of the Party . . . . Representative **Gerald R. Ford,** 50, of Michigan, reported that he would fight for leadership of Republicans in the House of Representatives against incumbent, 64-year-old Representative **Charles A. Halleck** of Indiana . . . . **Luther Hodges** resigned as Secretary of Commerce and was succeeded by John T. Connor, president of Merck & Co., one

...he world's largest pharmaceutical manufacturers.

Blaming political pressure by President Johnson, a Boston bank rescinded a rise in the basic interest rate . . . . **U.S. personal incomes** were reported (Dec. 18) to have exceeded a $500 billion annual rate for the first time. The report gave the annual rate as $502 billion.

A 3.5 bazooka shell fired (Dec. 11) at the United Nations building in New York fell short of its mark while **Major Ernesto Che Guevara,** Cuban Minister of Defense, was addressing the U.N. Assembly . . . . **The U.N. announced** (Dec. 4) that uniformed security guards were escorting late women workers to transportation facilities.

President Johnson announced (Dec. 18) that the U.S. would build a new sea-level canal at one of four sites, two in Panama, one in Colombia, and one on the border between Costa Rica and Nicaragua.

An estimated 100,000 people had to abandon their homes (Dec. 6) in upper New York State in bitter winter weather after an ice storm snapped power lines . . . . Because of heavy snows, **eight Montana counties** were designated (Dec. 19) a disaster area by President Johnson . . . . On December 22, the **State of Oregon and four counties in California** were classed as disaster areas following snow, rain and floods . . . . At least 11 people died in Idaho as a result of the worst floods in years . . . . Fire caused (Dec. 19) more than $5 million worth of damage in **Neiman-Marcus,** famed Dallas (Tex.) department store.

Three bandits in **Patterson, N.J.,** robbed a bank truck of more than $500,000 after hiding in an adjacent rectory and tying up four priests.

First Medal of Honor in Viet Nam fighting was awarded (Dec. 3) to army captain **Roger Hugh L. Donlon** of Saugerties, N.Y.

INTERNATIONAL

Leaving India (Dec. 4) after a three-day visit, **Pope Paul VI** called on the nations of the world to pool even a small part of their defense expenditures in a fund to provide food, clothing, shelter and medical care for developing countries.

Gustavo Diaz Ordaz inaugurated (Dec. 1) as President of Mexico, succeeding Adolfo Lopez Mateos.

Col. Juan Peron, former dictator of Argentina, was halted in Brazil while en route back to Argentina and returned to Spain where he has maintained his residence since being ousted as ruler of his native country . . . . **Cuba's Minister of Labor,** 46-year-old Augusto Martinez shot himself after being fired from his post . . . . **President Antonio Segni** of Italy resigned (Dec. 6) as result of declining health following a stroke during the summer . . . . **Kenya** became the latest African republic (Dec. 12) under President Jomo Kenyatta . . . . **Forbes Burnham** replaced leftist Cheddi B. Jagan as Premier of British Guiana.

The Soviet Union sent arms to rebel forces in the former Belgian Congo (Dec. 6). The move was interpreted as aimed at undercutting the influence of Red China with the rebels . . . . **Premier Moise Tshombe** of the Congo 'reappropriated' all mining concessions in his country announcing that he would sell rights to exploit the mines to the highest bidders.

President Charles de Gaulle of France threatened to cancel the Treaty of Mutual Cooperation with West Germany if that country signed a Multi-Nuclear Force pact with the U.S.

Buddhist leaders in S. Viet Nam agreed (Dec. 10) to try to overthrow the regime of Premier Tran Van Huong . . . . Three Buddhist leaders began fasting as a protest against the Tran Van Huong government . . . . **The S. Viet Nam Military Council** assumed (Dec. 19) a veto over the civilian government of Premier Huong . . . . **Rejecting protests by the U.S.,** Lt. Gen. Nguyen Khan, military strong man of S. Viet Nam, asserted (Dec. 22) the right of the military to overrule the civilian government.

Britain's House of Commons by a vote of 355-170 called for abolition of the death penalty (Dec. 21).

SPORTS

The Baltimore Colts won the championship of the Western Conference of the National Football League. The Cleveland Browns took the Eastern Conference title. In the national title contest Cleveland defeated Baltimore 27-0.

In the American Football League, San Diego led the Western Division, the Buffalo Bills the Eastern Division. Buffalo took the national title by defeating San Diego by a score of 20-7.

Joey Giardello successfully defended his middleweight boxing title by outpointing (Dec. 14) Rubin Carter.

OBITUARIES

William Bendix, film and television star, in Los Angeles, aged 58.

12/2/64 – Official portrait of LBJ's youngest, Luci Baines Johnson, who will reign as Azalea Festival queen in 1965.

NATIONAL NEWS

12/1/64 – Dr. Sam Sheppard, who was convicted of his wife's murder and served ten years, won motion for new trial, granted freedom. Sheppard and present wife put record collection in order in livingroom of Bay City home.

12/2/64 – Dr. Martin Luther King, Jr. leaves Federal Bureau of Investigation after conferring with FBI Director J. Edgar Hoover. King requested conference in wake of verbal feud climaxed by Hoover's statement that Nobel Peace Prize winner was "most notorious liar in the country."

12/2/64 – Controversial Washington figure, Robert G. Baker, appearing before Senate Rules Committee, once again refused to answer questions concerning his private manipulations while he was Senate Democratic secretary.

STUDENT "FREE SPEECH MOVEMENT"

12/2/64 – One thousand students from University of California at Berkeley staged a mass sit-in during a "free speech" demonstration. In addition to objecting to rules governing political activity on campus, they demanded ouster of President and Chancellor.

12/7/64 — Above, Mario Savio (arrow), leader of Univ. of Cal. rebel student "free speech movement," addresses some of the 768 individuals arrested 12/3 during demonstration at Sproul Hall. Savio spoke as they gathered for arraignment in temporary court set up in Berkeley's Community Theatre. He said he looked with profound disfavor on peace plan to be presented to an "extraordinary convocation" of students and faculty. Left, policeman books barefoot girl at scene of sit-in.

12/3/64 — Harlem councilman, J. Raymond Jones, tells wife good news after his election as N.Y. County Democratic leader making him boss of Tammany Hall and third most powerful Democrat in the State. Nicknamed "The Fox," Jones became the first Negro to hold the important post.

12/3/64 — Janet Perring, 15, from Leroy, Ill., sobs on father's shoulder after her steer "Charger," Grand Champion of International Livestock Show in Chicago, was auctioned off for $17.50 a pound to the Stock Yards Packing Co. who placed bid for Central National Bank of Chicago. Prized animal weighed 1020 pounds.

12/5/64 — President Johnson pins Medal of Honor on Army Captain Roger Donlon for heroism in S. Viet Nam. Donlon is first winner of highest award since Korean War.

MERIDIAN MISSISSIPPI

12/8/64 — 19 persons charged with conspiracy in slaying of 3 civil rights workers on June 21, including Neshoba County Sheriff Lawrence Rainey and Deputy Cecil

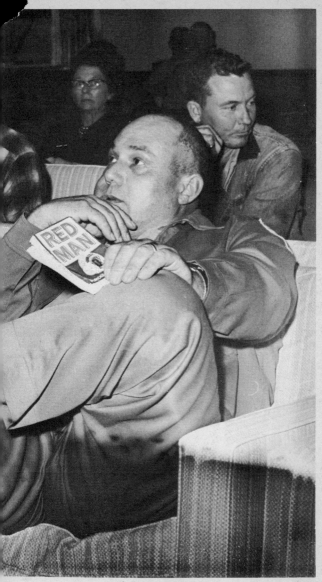

Price (above), were released 12/10 when U.S. Commissioner Esther Carter dropped charges. Another Commissioner in Biloxi released a 20th defendant.

12/10/64 — Commissioner sides — soon dropped charge against the 19. FBI stated 10 of 1 charged with conspiracy actuall took part in the slaying of Andre Goodman, Michael Schwerne and James Chaney.

12/10/64 — Mrs. Fannie Lee Cha ney (left), mother of one of thre slain civil rights workers, attende conspiracy hearings, hear charges dropped.

12/6/64 — Upper N. Y. State wa hit by one of worst ice storms i recent years. In Schenectad alone 50,000 homes were withou power. Governor Rockefeller de clared state of emergency.

12/9/64 — President Johnson, Rus sian Foreign Minister Andrei A Gromyko and Soviet Ambassado Anatoly Dobrynin struggle through a one hour and twent minute meeting at White House Discussion, which was described a friendly, produced little.

12/8/64 — Senator Edward (Ted) Kennedy, who said he'd be out of hospital by Christmas, took first steps in 6 months when visited by father in Boston.

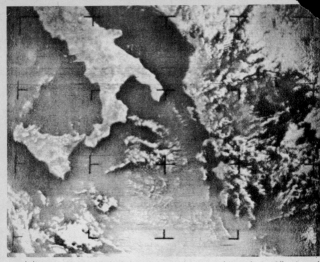

12/9/64 — Italy and Sicily show clearly, as do coasts of Yugoslavia, Albania and Greece, in automatic picture transmission photo taken from NASA's Nimbus I Meteorological Satellite and received by the French APT ground station near Lannion.

12/12/64 — A "rain" of spent shell casings drop from Navy's A4 Jet attack plane which is capable of delivering a concentration of 12,600 rounds of armor-piercing cannon shells per minute.

12/13/64 — Ieoh Ming Pei, 47-year-old naturalized American architect born in Canton, China, was commissioned to design the John F. Kennedy Memorial Library to be erected in Cambridge, Mass. Senator-elect Robert Kennedy announced that public contributions had exceeded 10 million. (Opposite) Mrs. Kennedy, escorted by U.N. Ambassador Stevenson, attended annual U.N. concert in General Assembly Hall.

12/16/64 – Senator Edward
nedy of Mass. leaves hospital with
wife Joan after 6-month stay due
to broken back suffered in plane
crash. Below, Ted, Jr. and sister
Kara, wait father's arrival at West
Palm Beach airport. Opposite
page, the Senator receives a big
welcome after deplaning.

TED KENNEDY LEAVES HOSPITAL

12/16/64 – Federal Aviation medical experts, researching a pilot's physiological age as opposed to his chronological years, test the finest subject to date, 90-year-old active airman, Dr. A. M. Wallace of Fate City, Va. According to FAA Dr. Wallace is probably the oldest active pilot in the world.

12/18/64 – Nobel Peace Prize winner, Dr. Martin Luther King, is guest at luncheon given by New York's Governor Rockefeller. L-R: Jackie Robinson; Mrs. Rockefeller; King; Rockefeller; Mrs. Coretta King; Mrs. Jackie Robinson; Mrs. Martin Luther King, Sr., and Martin Luther King, Sr.

12/22/64 – Worst floodwaters recent years brought death and destruction to Oregon, four counties in northern California and extensive areas in Idaho. National Guards of all three states were called up. Left, typical scene on Foster Rd. in S.E. Portland, Ore.

12/25/64 – 1964 Christmas Cards from the Nation's First Family show the White House lawn as painted in watercolor by artist Robert Laessig. In foreground are two oaks planted by the Johnsons, and in background the girls with the dogs.

12/24/64 – Reed Robertson, 13, (R) holds basketball, a gift of Mrs. Lyndon B. Johnson who visited family last spring on her tour of poverty stricken area in eastern Kentucky near Jackson. (L-R) Ray, 8, Mrs. Robertson, 34, Eugene, 12, Leslie, 7, Judy Ann, 5, Ronnie, 10. Standing, Mr. Arthur Robertson, 37, Roy, 14 and Reed.

NATIONAL NEWS-END

12/1/64 — Ghana Ambassador Alex Quaison-Sackey (center), newly-elected President of the 19th General Assembly of the United Nations, presides over December 1st session. Long-threatened showdown between U.S. and USSR over latter's unpaid assessments was postponed until Assembly concluded its general debate.

12/2/64 — Brazilian officials wait at of landing ramp in Rio De Janeiro to seize former Argentine dictator Juan Peron (arrow) after latter's surprise flight from Madrid in abortive attempt to return to Buenos Aires. Peron, now 69, was put on plane back to Spain.

12/3/64 — Pope Paul VI, the first Roman Catholic pontiff ever to visit the Orient, extends hands in greetings to some of the more than one million Indians who lined his route upon arrival in Bombay, India, for Eucharistic Congress. Addressing crowd, Pope Paul said: "We do not feel a stranger among you."

12/4/64 — Police reinforcements arrive on scene to disperse Communist mob which ransacked United States Information Service Library in Djakarta, Indonesia. Hundreds of youths smashed windows, doors to the Library in protest against American-Belgian mercy mission in The Congo. Similar riots occurred elsewhere in world, chiefly provoked by Communists. Later, U.S. announced it would close Djakarta Library.

12/8/64 — Congolese rebel leader Gaston Soumialot popped up in Cairo after his troops were driven from Stanleyville, and shook hands with Mrs. Pauline Lumumba, widow of The Congo's first Premier. Lumumba, who was murdered, has become spirit behind Communist-backed rebellion in the African state.

12/9/64 — Chilian President Eduardo Frei (left) watches Justice Minister Pedro Rodriguez sign proposed Constitutional reform which expands power of the Government, and the President, in Santiago.

BRITISH GUIANA

12/7/64 — Forbes Burnham picks way through members of his People's National Congress Party in Georgetown, British Guiana, election eve. A moderate Socialist, he joined right-wing group to oust Marxist Premier Cheddi Jagan. (See next page.)

12/7/64 – Cheddi Jagan, leftist Premier of British Guiana, who won 45 per cent of vote in election, refused to resign when British Governor General asked Jagan's opponents to form coalition government headed by Georgetown lawyer Forbes Burnham (see previous page). London pressure eased Jagan out 12/18.

12/9/64 – Premier Alexei Kosygin addresses session of the Supreme Soviet which unanimously approved him as successor to Nikita Khrushchev, who, though entitled to seat in the body, did not attend. Kosygin announced Russia's 1965 military budget would be cut half billion dollars.

12/20/64 – Italian Communist Party member Bruno Gombi, a member of that nation's Parliament, wipes blood from face after he and other party members clashed with police in demonstration against arrival in Rome of Congolese Premier Moise Tshombe.

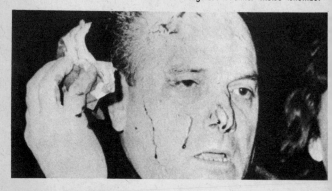

12/10/64 – Rev. Martin Luther King receives Nobel Peace Prize from Gunnar Jahn, chairman of prize committee, in Oslo. King, youngest man ever to receive the award, accepted it on behalf of American civil rights movement, saying that he was convinced non-violence was the only way in which significant progress could be made.

2/14/64 – Bearded Cuban Minister of
Industry Ernesto "Che" Guevara puffs on
cigar, eyes photographer as he arrives
for television appearance in New York.
Three days before, he denounced America
before U.N. General Assembly, while,
across river, Cuban freedom fighters
launched bazooka shell from home-made
mortar. It fell harmlessly in East River. Outside U.N. building, Cubans demonstrated,
one woman breaking through police lines,
armed with knife, to assassinate Guevara

BAZOOKA SHELL FIRED AT
UNITED NATIONS HEADQUARTERS

12/11/64 — On Queens lot across East River from U.N. building, police find mortar (mounted in milk crate), complete with eye-piece sight and electronic firing device, used unsuccessfully by persons unknown to bomb UN while Cuba's Guevara addressed Assembly. Left, 3 suspects are booked after arrest Dec. 22: L-R, Ignacio Novo; detective; Carlos Perez; Guillermo Novo.

12/14/64 — At former Auschwitz camp's wall of death, German war crimes officials determine if witnesses at far away windows could have seen shooting of prisoners by SS guards. The answer? Yes.

12/14/64 — President Jomo Kenyatta, former Mau-Mau leader, (on throne in rear) reads speech at opening of first Kenya National Assembly since his nation broke last link with British Commonwealth and became a republic on Dec. 11.

NEW ATLANTIC-PACIFIC LINK

12/18/64 — In a surprise announcement from the White House President Johnson "liquidated" the dispute with Panama over the Canal. The Chief Executive said the U.S. would proceed with plans for a new canal, without locks and larger; and that it would negotiate a new treaty for the present canal. President Robles of Panama hailed the proposal as an "historic . . . and happy moment," the end of the "in perpetuity" clause of the 1903 treaty and equally important, the end of the infringement of Panama's sovereignty. Top photo shows the "Big Ditch" in 1904 during the excavation of Gaillard Cut. Middle photo, shows locks which limit capacity of Canal to 60 ships per day, and which make it impossible for many U.S. naval vessels to get through at all. Bottom photo, map of four possible sites for new canal: two in Panama (including present one); one in Columbia and one along the Nicaragua-Costa Rica border. Most important factor: a nuclear attack could put present canal (with locks) out of commission for perhaps 6-7 years; a sea-level canal would be out of business for only a couple of weeks.

12/18/64 — Nguyen van Quy, 11, chews gum and inspects army binoculars after being coaxed into pointing out to S. Viet Nam troops the entrances to a network of tunnels used by Viet Cong forces. Lt. Col. Nguyen van Chuyen will adopt youth.

2/15/64 — Mrs. Florian Roule, the former Marie Dionne, one of our surviving quintuplets, appeared in court to answer charges of common assault.

2/17/64 — A 48-hour general strike was called by Argentina's pro-Peron Labor Federation. Downtown Buenos Aires was unaffected, but in outlying districts shots were fired at trains, molotov cocktails hurled at buses. Policeman wrestles Peronist for whip.

12/21/64 — Mrs. Pamela Mboya, wife of Kenya's Minister of Justice, Tom Mboya, presents a "speech day" prize, an encyclopedia, to high school student in Nairobi.

, 64 — Former President of Bolivia, Victor Paz Estenssoro, his wife the international beauty, Marie Teresa, and two of their daughters enjoy an afternoon at beach in Lima, Peru. A military coup last November 5th overthrew his government, forced him to flee to friendlier atmosphere.

2/23/64 — Tied up to mid-ocean TV tower, Dutch Coast Guard ship, Delfshaven, idles while police cut off power of "TV NORTH SEA." The station was accused of transmitting illegally to the Netherlands. Operators of the tower thought they were safely outside Dutch territorial waters. Authorities had other ideas—the matter will be decided in court.

2/27/64 — Dr. Carlos Sandico, Jr., addresses 3000 citizens of Angeles City, Philippines who were demonstrating against alleged killing of 31 of their countrymen by U.S. servicemen at American bases. U.S. Ambassador McCormick Blair, Jr., and Philippine President Macapagal discussed seriousness of situation.

INTERNATIONAL NEWS-END

12/8/64 — Delectable Shirley McLaine serves up tasty tid-bit in movie "John Gold-farb, Please Come Home" to actors posing as Notre Dame football team. Scene is in harem, night before game between Fighting Irish and Arab grid team. School officials won injunction against release of film in that permission from University was not granted and that team is portrayed as "gluttons and drunks."

12/3/64 — Real-life Notre Dame quarterback John Huarte receives Heisman Trophy as nation's top college player.

12/3/64 — Singer Ronie Rae before (left) and after alleged incident at actor Steve Cochran's Hollywood home. She signed complaint charging Cochran with false imprisonment; said she was invited to home, they quarreled, she was bound and gagged.

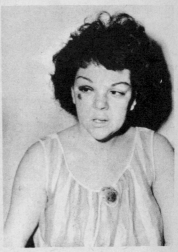

12/4/64 — Recovering nicely from the world's most highly-publicized tonsilectomy, Beatle drummer Ringo Starr greets his favorite fan, his mother, in London hospital. Bulletins concerning teen-age idol's condition were regularly released by officials to anxious hordes of Beatle boosters around the globe.

12/8/64 — World's fastest human, Florida A & M's Bob Hayes, gold medal winner at Tokyo Olympic Games, signs professional football contract with Dallas Cowboys of National Football League. Hayes' coach Jake Gaither (left) looks on.

12/8/64 — Actress Anna Kashfi, ex-wife of Marlon Brando, shows bruises after release from jail. She allegedly assaulted policeman after child custody papers were served.

12/14/64 — Middleweight cham Joey Giardello takes left from Ru bin Carter in Philadelphia titl fight. Giardello won.

12/3/64 — V-cut became an inverted-A when Paris designer Maggy Rouff unveiled her "almost topless" look in holiday evening wear. Gown plunges to the waist in front, but features a bead-and-sequin bra which matches elbow length sleeves.

12/11/64 — Boston Celtic's Bill Russell restrains fan who became involved in rhubarb with referee during intermission of Boston-Philadelphia 76er's game. Russell broke up the fracas. Next game, the all-time great scored his 10,000th point.

12/18/64 — Government representative holds back curious, including goateed boyfriend Bob Zaguri, as Brigitte Bardot arrives at Rio's airport for month of rest with Zaguri at nearby beach resort, Cabo Frio.

12/15/64 — Wilt Chamberlain, below, of San Francisco Warriors (wearing head gear) is fouled by N.Y. Knickerbockers' Willis Reed. Year-end newspaper columns were filled with speculation on Chamberlain being traded to New York.

12/14/64 — Cafe society congregates at New York's El Morocco, for the official opening of the famed supper club under the ownership of London's John Mills. A few of the "set" on hand were (L-R): Odile Rodin, French actress, and husband Porfirio Rubirosa, Mrs. Denniston Slater and actress Constance Bennett.

12/1/64 — Rumors in the German press to the contrary, ex-Empress Soraya of Iran and German actor Maximilian Schell are still very much paired in public.

12/6/64 — Playing at Kaanapali, Maui, the United States, represented by Jack Nicklaus and Arnold Palmer, won the Canada Cup for the 5th straight year. Nicklaus scored 276 and Palmer 278 for a record team total of 554. Nicklaus, above, receives Individual Trophy.

12/13/64 — Actress Anna Kashfi and 6-year-old son Christian greet each other as he arrives for court appointed day-long visit at her home. Earlier in the week child was remanded to custody of father Marlon Brando pending custody hearing. Actress Kashfi was involved in Bel Air hotel fracas 12/8 (see page 368).

12/18/64 — Latest creation of Salvador Dali involves a couple of incinerated lovers in a charred bed. Dali thought it lacked fire, decided to surround wire-framed dummies with straw, ignite the whole deal as a "happening" or visual thrill show. Scheme misfired when students of Paris Am. Students Assoc. failed to provide enough straw. Mr. Dali told them to go to blazes, stormed off the grounds.

12/21/64 — Actor Rex Harrison (L) chats with actress Audrey Hepburn (R) and husband Mel Ferrer (C) at Paris premiere of movie "My Fair Lady" in which Hepburn and Harrison star.

12/22/64 — Hollywood stunt men were unavailable for the shooting of an MGM movie in Spain. As a result actors on the set assumed the hazardous risks of trick riding.

12/27/64 — Cleveland Browns' quarterback, Frank Ryan, takes well-deserved shower after leading team to N.F.L. Championship by whipping Baltimore Colts 27-0. On previous day the Buffalo Bills defeated the San Diego Chargers to win A.F.L. crown. During season, Cleveland fullback, Jim Brown, established himself more than ever as greatest runner of all time by gaining 1446 yards, leading N.F.L. seventh time in eight seasons and increasing career total to 10,768 yards and 105 TD's.

**ENTERTAINMENT
SPORTS & THE ARTS
END**

12/12/64 — Ernest Ferrell slides to ground in Nashville, Tenn., as he is hit by 4,400 volts of electricity. Power line fell across his truck. He died.

MISCELLANY

12/9/64 — Expert spelunker (explorer of caves) Antoine Senni receives farewell kiss from his wife before descending alone to explore unknown depths of cave-system in France. He plans to remain underground four months.

12/12/64 — Sister Stephen, an Ursuline nun, at left in her normal habit and at right in new religious garb approved by her superior as a pilot project in Oklahoma City. New habit features skirt, long-sleeved blouse and weskit with insignia of her order. Reaction of students was favorable.

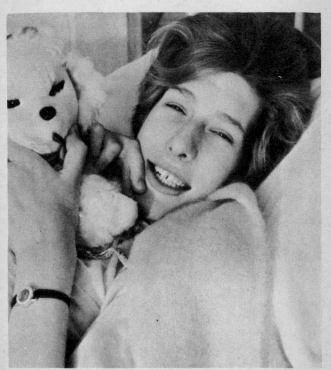

12/21/64 — Auburn-haired Ann Rowston of Hyde, Cheshire, England, who is 19 and 6 feet 7 inches tall, is undergoing a series of operations to reduce her height by 6 inches. A patient at the Oswestry Orthopedic Hospital for four months, she has already undergone three successful operations for bone removal from her legs.

12/18/64 — Hotelman Glynn Wolfe, 50, affectionately tweaks ear of bride-to-be, Demerle Rankin Wolfe, 18, of Pasco, Wash., after they took out marriage license in Los Angeles, Cal. Wolfe, who is also an ordained minister, will be taking on bride #17. Demerle Rankin was #16, divorced him 3 weeks ago, decided to try again.

12/17/64 — Students, members of USC's Phi Gamma Delta fraternity, pick up 1700 pound car in a Volks-tote Contest. Object of race is to lift car, carry it 100 yards, all carriers get in or on car, drive it back to finish line. A rough time is had by all.

12/22/64 — A lion mauls the dead body of animal keeper George Herzel, 50, (arrow at right) after 4 of the big cats escaped from circus cage in Adelaide, Australia. Police and professional hunters killed two lions and a lioness on carnival grounds. The fourth was lured back to its cage by the tamer who also owns circus.

12/21/64 — Able Seaman John Lukens (foreground) of Meuse, Pa., Third Mate Charles Jackson of New London, Conn., and Captain Frederick Mohle (sharing life preserver in background), abandoned the S.S. Voyager, picked up by Matilde Bolten. Freighter split seam and finally sank while being towed by British tug Marina.

12/21/64 — Isabelle Kainoa, 30, leaped 230 feet from the San Francisco-Oakland Bay Bridge and lived to tell the tale. She lies on stretcher after being picked up by U.S. Coast Guard.

12/31/64 — Officers and motorists dash from Los Angeles Freeway to get help in removing body and engine of car which smashed in two. Two college students miraculously escaped death. Anticipated deaths from highway accidents for year 1964: 48,000.

DECEMBER – END